CAREER EXAMINATION SERIES

D1739684

THIS IS YOUR **PASSBOOK**® FOR ...

ENVIRONMENTALIST

NLC®

NATIONAL LEARNING CORPORATION®
passbooks.com

Copyright © 2020 by

National Learning Corporation

212 Michael Drive, Syosset, NY 11791
(516) 921-8888 • www.passbooks.com
E-mail: info@passbooks.com

PUBLISHED IN THE UNITED STATES OF AMERICA

PASSBOOK® SERIES

THE *PASSBOOK® SERIES* has been created to prepare applicants and candidates for the ultimate academic battlefield – the examination room.

At some time in our lives, each and every one of us may be required to take an examination – for validation, matriculation, admission, qualification, registration, certification, or licensure.

Based on the assumption that every applicant or candidate has met the basic formal educational standards, has taken the required number of courses, and read the necessary texts, the *PASSBOOK® SERIES* furnishes the one special preparation which may assure passing with confidence, instead of failing with insecurity. Examination questions – together with answers – are furnished as the basic vehicle for study so that the mysteries of the examination and its compounding difficulties may be eliminated or diminished by a sure method.

This book is meant to help you pass your examination provided that you qualify and are serious in your objective.

The entire field is reviewed through the huge store of content information which is succinctly presented through a provocative and challenging approach – the question-and-answer method.

A climate of success is established by furnishing the correct answers at the end of each test.

You soon learn to recognize types of questions, forms of questions, and patterns of questioning. You may even begin to anticipate expected outcomes.

You perceive that many questions are repeated or adapted so that you can gain acute insights, which may enable you to score many sure points.

You learn how to confront new questions, or types of questions, and to attack them confidently and work out the correct answers.

You note objectives and emphases, and recognize pitfalls and dangers, so that you may make positive educational adjustments.

Moreover, you are kept fully informed in relation to new concepts, methods, practices, and directions in the field.

You discover that you arre actually taking the examination all the time: you are preparing for the examination by "taking" an examination, not by reading extraneous and/or supererogatory textbooks.

In short, this PASSBOOK®, used directedly, should be an important factor in helping you to pass your test.

ENVIRONMENTALIST

DUTIES

Assists in the detection, analysis, and research aspects of compliance with the provisions of local, state, and federal environmental regulations and codes. Participates in sampling and evaluating marine and surface waters, industrial and sanitary sewage treatment systems as well as other sources of environmental pollution. The training of the employee is provided by supervisors who assign progressively more difficult and responsible duties according to the trainee's experience and level of professional development. Performs related work as required.

SCOPE OF THE EXAMINATION

The written test will be designed to test for knowledge, skills, and/or abilities in such areas as:

1. Collection, analysis, and interpretation of data;
2. Preparing written material;
3. Elementary principles of biology, chemistry, and general science; and
4. Arithmetic, arithmetic reasoning, and basic statistics.

HOW TO TAKE A TEST

I. YOU MUST PASS AN EXAMINATION

A. *WHAT EVERY CANDIDATE SHOULD KNOW*

Examination applicants often ask us for help in preparing for the written test. What can I study in advance? What kinds of questions will be asked? How will the test be given? How will the papers be graded?

As an applicant for a civil service examination, you may be wondering about some of these things. Our purpose here is to suggest effective methods of advance study and to describe civil service examinations.

Your chances for success on this examination can be increased if you know how to prepare. Those "pre-examination jitters" can be reduced if you know what to expect. You can even experience an adventure in good citizenship if you know why civil service exams are given.

B. *WHY ARE CIVIL SERVICE EXAMINATIONS GIVEN?*

Civil service examinations are important to you in two ways. As a citizen, you want public jobs filled by employees who know how to do their work. As a job seeker, you want a fair chance to compete for that job on an equal footing with other candidates. The best-known means of accomplishing this two-fold goal is the competitive examination.

Exams are widely publicized throughout the nation. They may be administered for jobs in federal, state, city, municipal, town or village governments or agencies.

Any citizen may apply, with some limitations, such as the age or residence of applicants. Your experience and education may be reviewed to see whether you meet the requirements for the particular examination. When these requirements exist, they are reasonable and applied consistently to all applicants. Thus, a competitive examination may cause you some uneasiness now, but it is your privilege and safeguard.

C. *HOW ARE CIVIL SERVICE EXAMS DEVELOPED?*

Examinations are carefully written by trained technicians who are specialists in the field known as "psychological measurement," in consultation with recognized authorities in the field of work that the test will cover. These experts recommend the subject matter areas or skills to be tested; only those knowledges or skills important to your success on the job are included. The most reliable books and source materials available are used as references. Together, the experts and technicians judge the difficulty level of the questions.

Test technicians know how to phrase questions so that the problem is clearly stated. Their ethics do not permit "trick" or "catch" questions. Questions may have been tried out on sample groups, or subjected to statistical analysis, to determine their usefulness.

Written tests are often used in combination with performance tests, ratings of training and experience, and oral interviews. All of these measures combine to form the best-known means of finding the right person for the right job.

II. HOW TO PASS THE WRITTEN TEST

A. NATURE OF THE EXAMINATION

To prepare intelligently for civil service examinations, you should know how they differ from school examinations you have taken. In school you were assigned certain definite pages to read or subjects to cover. The examination questions were quite detailed and usually emphasized memory. Civil service exams, on the other hand, try to discover your present ability to perform the duties of a position, plus your potentiality to learn these duties. In other words, a civil service exam attempts to predict how successful you will be. Questions cover such a broad area that they cannot be as minute and detailed as school exam questions.

In the public service similar kinds of work, or positions, are grouped together in one "class." This process is known as *position-classification*. All the positions in a class are paid according to the salary range for that class. One class title covers all of these positions, and they are all tested by the same examination.

B. FOUR BASIC STEPS

1) Study the announcement

How, then, can you know what subjects to study? Our best answer is: "Learn as much as possible about the class of positions for which you've applied." The exam will test the knowledge, skills and abilities needed to do the work.

Your most valuable source of information about the position you want is the official exam announcement. This announcement lists the training and experience qualifications. Check these standards and apply only if you come reasonably close to meeting them.

The brief description of the position in the examination announcement offers some clues to the subjects which will be tested. Think about the job itself. Review the duties in your mind. Can you perform them, or are there some in which you are rusty? Fill in the blank spots in your preparation.

Many jurisdictions preview the written test in the exam announcement by including a section called "Knowledge and Abilities Required," "Scope of the Examination," or some similar heading. Here you will find out specifically what fields will be tested.

2) Review your own background

Once you learn in general what the position is all about, and what you need to know to do the work, ask yourself which subjects you already know fairly well and which need improvement. You may wonder whether to concentrate on improving your strong areas or on building some background in your fields of weakness. When the announcement has specified "some knowledge" or "considerable knowledge," or has used adjectives like "beginning principles of…" or "advanced … methods," you can get a clue as to the number and difficulty of questions to be asked in any given field. More questions, and hence broader coverage, would be included for those subjects which are more important in the work. Now weigh your strengths and weaknesses against the job requirements and prepare accordingly.

3) Determine the level of the position

Another way to tell how intensively you should prepare is to understand the level of the job for which you are applying. Is it the entering level? In other words, is this the position in which beginners in a field of work are hired? Or is it an intermediate or advanced level? Sometimes this is indicated by such words as "Junior" or "Senior" in the class title. Other jurisdictions use Roman numerals to designate the level – Clerk I, Clerk II, for example. The word "Supervisor" sometimes appears in the title. If the level is not indicated by the title, check the description of duties. Will you be working under very close supervision, or will you have responsibility for independent decisions in this work?

4) Choose appropriate study materials

Now that you know the subjects to be examined and the relative amount of each subject to be covered, you can choose suitable study materials. For beginning level jobs, or even advanced ones, if you have a pronounced weakness in some aspect of your training, read a modern, standard textbook in that field. Be sure it is up to date and has general coverage. Such books are normally available at your library, and the librarian will be glad to help you locate one. For entry-level positions, questions of appropriate difficulty are chosen – neither highly advanced questions, nor those too simple. Such questions require careful thought but not advanced training.

If the position for which you are applying is technical or advanced, you will read more advanced, specialized material. If you are already familiar with the basic principles of your field, elementary textbooks would waste your time. Concentrate on advanced textbooks and technical periodicals. Think through the concepts and review difficult problems in your field.

These are all general sources. You can get more ideas on your own initiative, following these leads. For example, training manuals and publications of the government agency which employs workers in your field can be useful, particularly for technical and professional positions. A letter or visit to the government department involved may result in more specific study suggestions, and certainly will provide you with a more definite idea of the exact nature of the position you are seeking.

III. KINDS OF TESTS

Tests are used for purposes other than measuring knowledge and ability to perform specified duties. For some positions, it is equally important to test ability to make adjustments to new situations or to profit from training. In others, basic mental abilities not dependent on information are essential. Questions which test these things may not appear as pertinent to the duties of the position as those which test for knowledge and information. Yet they are often highly important parts of a fair examination. For very general questions, it is almost impossible to help you direct your study efforts. What we can do is to point out some of the more common of these general abilities needed in public service positions and describe some typical questions.

1) General information

Broad, general information has been found useful for predicting job success in some kinds of work. This is tested in a variety of ways, from vocabulary lists to questions about current events. Basic background in some field of work, such as sociology or economics, may be sampled in a group of questions. Often these are principles which have become familiar to most persons through exposure rather than through formal training. It is difficult to advise you how to study for these questions; being alert to the world around you is our best suggestion.

2) Verbal ability

An example of an ability needed in many positions is verbal or language ability. Verbal ability is, in brief, the ability to use and understand words. Vocabulary and grammar tests are typical measures of this ability. Reading comprehension or paragraph interpretation questions are common in many kinds of civil service tests. You are given a paragraph of written material and asked to find its central meaning.

3) Numerical ability

Number skills can be tested by the familiar arithmetic problem, by checking paired lists of numbers to see which are alike and which are different, or by interpreting charts and graphs. In the latter test, a graph may be printed in the test booklet which you are asked to use as the basis for answering questions.

4) Observation

A popular test for law-enforcement positions is the observation test. A picture is shown to you for several minutes, then taken away. Questions about the picture test your ability to observe both details and larger elements.

5) Following directions

In many positions in the public service, the employee must be able to carry out written instructions dependably and accurately. You may be given a chart with several columns, each column listing a variety of information. The questions require you to carry out directions involving the information given in the chart.

6) Skills and aptitudes

Performance tests effectively measure some manual skills and aptitudes. When the skill is one in which you are trained, such as typing or shorthand, you can practice. These tests are often very much like those given in business school or high school courses. For many of the other skills and aptitudes, however, no short-time preparation can be made. Skills and abilities natural to you or that you have developed throughout your lifetime are being tested.

Many of the general questions just described provide all the data needed to answer the questions and ask you to use your reasoning ability to find the answers. Your best preparation for these tests, as well as for tests of facts and ideas, is to be at your physical and mental best. You, no doubt, have your own methods of getting into an exam-taking mood and keeping "in shape." The next section lists some ideas on this subject.

IV. KINDS OF QUESTIONS

Only rarely is the "essay" question, which you answer in narrative form, used in civil service tests. Civil service tests are usually of the short-answer type. Full instructions for answering these questions will be given to you at the examination. But in case this is your first experience with short-answer questions and separate answer sheets, here is what you need to know:

1) Multiple-choice Questions

Most popular of the short-answer questions is the "multiple choice" or "best answer" question. It can be used, for example, to test for factual knowledge, ability to solve problems or judgment in meeting situations found at work.

A multiple-choice question is normally one of three types—

- It can begin with an incomplete statement followed by several possible endings. You are to find the one ending which *best* completes the statement, although some of the others may not be entirely wrong.
- It can also be a complete statement in the form of a question which is answered by choosing one of the statements listed.
- It can be in the form of a problem – again you select the best answer.

Here is an example of a multiple-choice question with a discussion which should give you some clues as to the method for choosing the right answer:

When an employee has a complaint about his assignment, the action which will *best* help him overcome his difficulty is to
- A. discuss his difficulty with his coworkers
- B. take the problem to the head of the organization
- C. take the problem to the person who gave him the assignment
- D. say nothing to anyone about his complaint

In answering this question, you should study each of the choices to find which is best. Consider choice "A" – Certainly an employee may discuss his complaint with fellow employees, but no change or improvement can result, and the complaint remains unresolved. Choice "B" is a poor choice since the head of the organization probably does not know what assignment you have been given, and taking your problem to him is known as "going over the head" of the supervisor. The supervisor, or person who made the assignment, is the person who can clarify it or correct any injustice. Choice "C" is, therefore, correct. To say nothing, as in choice "D," is unwise. Supervisors have and interest in knowing the problems employees are facing, and the employee is seeking a solution to his problem.

2) True/False Questions

The "true/false" or "right/wrong" form of question is sometimes used. Here a complete statement is given. Your job is to decide whether the statement is right or wrong.

SAMPLE: A roaming cell-phone call to a nearby city costs less than a non-roaming call to a distant city.

This statement is wrong, or false, since roaming calls are more expensive.
This is not a complete list of all possible question forms, although most of the others are variations of these common types. You will always get complete directions for

answering questions. Be sure you understand *how* to mark your answers – ask questions until you do.

V. RECORDING YOUR ANSWERS

Computer terminals are used more and more today for many different kinds of exams.

For an examination with very few applicants, you may be told to record your answers in the test booklet itself. Separate answer sheets are much more common. If this separate answer sheet is to be scored by machine – and this is often the case – it is highly important that you mark your answers correctly in order to get credit.

An electronic scoring machine is often used in civil service offices because of the speed with which papers can be scored. Machine-scored answer sheets must be marked with a pencil, which will be given to you. This pencil has a high graphite content which responds to the electronic scoring machine. As a matter of fact, stray dots may register as answers, so do not let your pencil rest on the answer sheet while you are pondering the correct answer. Also, if your pencil lead breaks or is otherwise defective, ask for another.

Since the answer sheet will be dropped in a slot in the scoring machine, be careful not to bend the corners or get the paper crumpled.

The answer sheet normally has five vertical columns of numbers, with 30 numbers to a column. These numbers correspond to the question numbers in your test booklet. After each number, going across the page are four or five pairs of dotted lines. These short dotted lines have small letters or numbers above them. The first two pairs may also have a "T" or "F" above the letters. This indicates that the first two pairs only are to be used if the questions are of the true-false type. If the questions are multiple choice, disregard the "T" and "F" and pay attention only to the small letters or numbers.

Answer your questions in the manner of the sample that follows:

32. The largest city in the United States is
    A. Washington, D.C.
    B. New York City
    C. Chicago
    D. Detroit
    E. San Francisco

1) Choose the answer you think is best. (New York City is the largest, so "B" is correct.)
2) Find the row of dotted lines numbered the same as the question you are answering. (Find row number 32)
3) Find the pair of dotted lines corresponding to the answer. (Find the pair of lines under the mark "B.")
4) Make a solid black mark between the dotted lines.

VI. BEFORE THE TEST

Common sense will help you find procedures to follow to get ready for an examination. Too many of us, however, overlook these sensible measures. Indeed, nervousness and fatigue have been found to be the most serious reasons why applicants fail to do their best on civil service tests. Here is a list of reminders:

- Begin your preparation early – Don't wait until the last minute to go scurrying around for books and materials or to find out what the position is all about.
- Prepare continuously – An hour a night for a week is better than an all-night cram session. This has been definitely established. What is more, a night a week for a month will return better dividends than crowding your study into a shorter period of time.
- Locate the place of the exam – You have been sent a notice telling you when and where to report for the examination. If the location is in a different town or otherwise unfamiliar to you, it would be well to inquire the best route and learn something about the building.
- Relax the night before the test – Allow your mind to rest. Do not study at all that night. Plan some mild recreation or diversion; then go to bed early and get a good night's sleep.
- Get up early enough to make a leisurely trip to the place for the test – This way unforeseen events, traffic snarls, unfamiliar buildings, etc. will not upset you.
- Dress comfortably – A written test is not a fashion show. You will be known by number and not by name, so wear something comfortable.
- Leave excess paraphernalia at home – Shopping bags and odd bundles will get in your way. You need bring only the items mentioned in the official notice you received; usually everything you need is provided. Do not bring reference books to the exam. They will only confuse those last minutes and be taken away from you when in the test room.
- Arrive somewhat ahead of time – If because of transportation schedules you must get there very early, bring a newspaper or magazine to take your mind off yourself while waiting.
- Locate the examination room – When you have found the proper room, you will be directed to the seat or part of the room where you will sit. Sometimes you are given a sheet of instructions to read while you are waiting. Do not fill out any forms until you are told to do so; just read them and be prepared.
- Relax and prepare to listen to the instructions
- If you have any physical problem that may keep you from doing your best, be sure to tell the test administrator. If you are sick or in poor health, you really cannot do your best on the exam. You can come back and take the test some other time.

VII. AT THE TEST

The day of the test is here and you have the test booklet in your hand. The temptation to get going is very strong. Caution! There is more to success than knowing the right answers. You must know how to identify your papers and understand variations in the type of short-answer question used in this particular examination. Follow these suggestions for maximum results from your efforts:

1) Cooperate with the monitor

The test administrator has a duty to create a situation in which you can be as much at ease as possible. He will give instructions, tell you when to begin, check to see that you are marking your answer sheet correctly, and so on. He is not there to guard you, although he will see that your competitors do not take unfair advantage. He wants to help you do your best.

2) Listen to all instructions

Don't jump the gun! Wait until you understand all directions. In most civil service tests you get more time than you need to answer the questions. So don't be in a hurry. Read each word of instructions until you clearly understand the meaning. Study the examples, listen to all announcements and follow directions. Ask questions if you do not understand what to do.

3) Identify your papers

Civil service exams are usually identified by number only. You will be assigned a number; you must not put your name on your test papers. Be sure to copy your number correctly. Since more than one exam may be given, copy your exact examination title.

4) Plan your time

Unless you are told that a test is a "speed" or "rate of work" test, speed itself is usually not important. Time enough to answer all the questions will be provided, but this does not mean that you have all day. An overall time limit has been set. Divide the total time (in minutes) by the number of questions to determine the approximate time you have for each question.

5) Do not linger over difficult questions

If you come across a difficult question, mark it with a paper clip (useful to have along) and come back to it when you have been through the booklet. One caution if you do this – be sure to skip a number on your answer sheet as well. Check often to be sure that you have not lost your place and that you are marking in the row numbered the same as the question you are answering.

6) Read the questions

Be sure you know what the question asks! Many capable people are unsuccessful because they failed to *read* the questions correctly.

7) Answer all questions

Unless you have been instructed that a penalty will be deducted for incorrect answers, it is better to guess than to omit a question.

8) Speed tests

It is often better NOT to guess on speed tests. It has been found that on timed tests people are tempted to spend the last few seconds before time is called in marking answers at random – without even reading them – in the hope of picking up a few extra points. To discourage this practice, the instructions may warn you that your score will be "corrected" for guessing. That is, a penalty will be applied. The incorrect answers will be deducted from the correct ones, or some other penalty formula will be used.

9) Review your answers

If you finish before time is called, go back to the questions you guessed or omitted to give them further thought. Review other answers if you have time.

10) Return your test materials

If you are ready to leave before others have finished or time is called, take ALL your materials to the monitor and leave quietly. Never take any test material with you. The monitor can discover whose papers are not complete, and taking a test booklet may be grounds for disqualification.

VIII. EXAMINATION TECHNIQUES

1) Read the general instructions carefully. These are usually printed on the first page of the exam booklet. As a rule, these instructions refer to the timing of the examination; the fact that you should not start work until the signal and must stop work at a signal, etc. If there are any *special* instructions, such as a choice of questions to be answered, make sure that you note this instruction carefully.

2) When you are ready to start work on the examination, that is as soon as the signal has been given, read the instructions to each question booklet, underline any key words or phrases, such as *least, best, outline, describe* and the like. In this way you will tend to answer as requested rather than discover on reviewing your paper that you *listed without describing*, that you selected the *worst* choice rather than the *best* choice, etc.

3) If the examination is of the objective or multiple-choice type – that is, each question will also give a series of possible answers: A, B, C or D, and you are called upon to select the best answer and write the letter next to that answer on your answer paper – it is advisable to start answering each question in turn. There may be anywhere from 50 to 100 such questions in the three or four hours allotted and you can see how much time would be taken if you read through all the questions before beginning to answer any. Furthermore, if you come across a question or group of questions which you know would be difficult to answer, it would undoubtedly affect your handling of all the other questions.

4) If the examination is of the essay type and contains but a few questions, it is a moot point as to whether you should read all the questions before starting to answer any one. Of course, if you are given a choice – say five out of seven and the like – then it is essential to read all the questions so you can eliminate the two that are most difficult. If, however, you are asked to answer all the questions, there may be danger in trying to answer the easiest one first because you may find that you will spend too much time on it. The best technique is to answer the first question, then proceed to the second, etc.

5) Time your answers. Before the exam begins, write down the time it started, then add the time allowed for the examination and write down the time it must be completed, then divide the time available somewhat as follows:

- If 3-1/2 hours are allowed, that would be 210 minutes. If you have 80 objective-type questions, that would be an average of 2-1/2 minutes per question. Allow yourself no more than 2 minutes per question, or a total of 160 minutes, which will permit about 50 minutes to review.
- If for the time allotment of 210 minutes there are 7 essay questions to answer, that would average about 30 minutes a question. Give yourself only 25 minutes per question so that you have about 35 minutes to review.

6) The most important instruction is to *read each question* and make sure you know what is wanted. The second most important instruction is to *time yourself properly* so that you answer every question. The third most important instruction is to *answer every question*. Guess if you have to but include something for each question. Remember that you will receive no credit for a blank and will probably receive some credit if you write something in answer to an essay question. If you guess a letter – say "B" for a multiple-choice question – you may have guessed right. If you leave a blank as an answer to a multiple-choice question, the examiners may respect your feelings but it will not add a point to your score. Some exams may penalize you for wrong answers, so in such cases *only*, you may not want to guess unless you have some basis for your answer.

7) Suggestions
   a. Objective-type questions
      1. Examine the question booklet for proper sequence of pages and questions
      2. Read all instructions carefully
      3. Skip any question which seems too difficult; return to it after all other questions have been answered
      4. Apportion your time properly; do not spend too much time on any single question or group of questions
      5. Note and underline key words – *all, most, fewest, least, best, worst, same, opposite,* etc.
      6. Pay particular attention to negatives
      7. Note unusual option, e.g., unduly long, short, complex, different or similar in content to the body of the question
      8. Observe the use of "hedging" words – *probably, may, most likely,* etc.
      9. Make sure that your answer is put next to the same number as the question
      10. Do not second-guess unless you have good reason to believe the second answer is definitely more correct
      11. Cross out original answer if you decide another answer is more accurate; do not erase until you are ready to hand your paper in
      12. Answer all questions; guess unless instructed otherwise
      13. Leave time for review

   b. Essay questions
      1. Read each question carefully
      2. Determine exactly what is wanted. Underline key words or phrases.
      3. Decide on outline or paragraph answer

4. Include many different points and elements unless asked to develop any one or two points or elements
5. Show impartiality by giving pros and cons unless directed to select one side only
6. Make and write down any assumptions you find necessary to answer the questions
7. Watch your English, grammar, punctuation and choice of words
8. Time your answers; don't crowd material

8) Answering the essay question

Most essay questions can be answered by framing the specific response around several key words or ideas. Here are a few such key words or ideas:

M's: manpower, materials, methods, money, management
P's: purpose, program, policy, plan, procedure, practice, problems, pitfalls, personnel, public relations
   a. Six basic steps in handling problems:
     1. Preliminary plan and background development
     2. Collect information, data and facts
     3. Analyze and interpret information, data and facts
     4. Analyze and develop solutions as well as make recommendations
     5. Prepare report and sell recommendations
     6. Install recommendations and follow up effectiveness

   b. Pitfalls to avoid
     1. *Taking things for granted* – A statement of the situation does not necessarily imply that each of the elements is necessarily true; for example, a complaint may be invalid and biased so that all that can be taken for granted is that a complaint has been registered
     2. *Considering only one side of a situation* – Wherever possible, indicate several alternatives and then point out the reasons you selected the best one
     3. *Failing to indicate follow up* – Whenever your answer indicates action on your part, make certain that you will take proper follow-up action to see how successful your recommendations, procedures or actions turn out to be
     4. *Taking too long in answering any single question* – Remember to time your answers properly

IX. AFTER THE TEST

Scoring procedures differ in detail among civil service jurisdictions although the general principles are the same. Whether the papers are hand-scored or graded by machine we have described, they are nearly always graded by number. That is, the person who marks the paper knows only the number – never the name – of the applicant. Not until all the papers have been graded will they be matched with names. If other tests, such as training and experience or oral interview ratings have been given, scores will be combined. Different parts of the examination usually have different weights. For example, the written test might count 60 percent of the final grade, and a rating of training and experience 40 percent. In many jurisdictions, veterans will have a certain number of points added to their grades.

After the final grade has been determined, the names are placed in grade order and an eligible list is established. There are various methods for resolving ties between those who get the same final grade – probably the most common is to place first the name of the person whose application was received first. Job offers are made from the eligible list in the order the names appear on it. You will be notified of your grade and your rank as soon as all these computations have been made. This will be done as rapidly as possible.

People who are found to meet the requirements in the announcement are called "eligibles." Their names are put on a list of eligible candidates. An eligible's chances of getting a job depend on how high he stands on this list and how fast agencies are filling jobs from the list.

When a job is to be filled from a list of eligibles, the agency asks for the names of people on the list of eligibles for that job. When the civil service commission receives this request, it sends to the agency the names of the three people highest on this list. Or, if the job to be filled has specialized requirements, the office sends the agency the names of the top three persons who meet these requirements from the general list.

The appointing officer makes a choice from among the three people whose names were sent to him. If the selected person accepts the appointment, the names of the others are put back on the list to be considered for future openings.

That is the rule in hiring from all kinds of eligible lists, whether they are for typist, carpenter, chemist, or something else. For every vacancy, the appointing officer has his choice of any one of the top three eligibles on the list. This explains why the person whose name is on top of the list sometimes does not get an appointment when some of the persons lower on the list do. If the appointing officer chooses the second or third eligible, the No. 1 eligible does not get a job at once, but stays on the list until he is appointed or the list is terminated.

X. HOW TO PASS THE INTERVIEW TEST

The examination for which you applied requires an oral interview test. You have already taken the written test and you are now being called for the interview test – the final part of the formal examination.

You may think that it is not possible to prepare for an interview test and that there are no procedures to follow during an interview. Our purpose is to point out some things you can do in advance that will help you and some good rules to follow and pitfalls to avoid while you are being interviewed.

What is an interview supposed to test?
The written examination is designed to test the technical knowledge and competence of the candidate; the oral is designed to evaluate intangible qualities, not readily measured otherwise, and to establish a list showing the relative fitness of each candidate – as measured against his competitors – for the position sought. Scoring is not on the basis of "right" and "wrong," but on a sliding scale of values ranging from "not passable" to "outstanding." As a matter of fact, it is possible to achieve a relatively low score without a single "incorrect" answer because of evident weakness in the qualities being measured.

Occasionally, an examination may consist entirely of an oral test – either an individual or a group oral. In such cases, information is sought concerning the technical knowledges and abilities of the candidate, since there has been no written examination for this purpose. More commonly, however, an oral test is used to supplement a written examination.

Who conducts interviews?

The composition of oral boards varies among different jurisdictions. In nearly all, a representative of the personnel department serves as chairman. One of the members of the board may be a representative of the department in which the candidate would work. In some cases, "outside experts" are used, and, frequently, a businessman or some other representative of the general public is asked to serve. Labor and management or other special groups may be represented. The aim is to secure the services of experts in the appropriate field.

However the board is composed, it is a good idea (and not at all improper or unethical) to ascertain in advance of the interview who the members are and what groups they represent. When you are introduced to them, you will have some idea of their backgrounds and interests, and at least you will not stutter and stammer over their names.

What should be done before the interview?

While knowledge about the board members is useful and takes some of the surprise element out of the interview, there is other preparation which is more substantive. It *is* possible to prepare for an oral interview – in several ways:

1) Keep a copy of your application and review it carefully before the interview

This may be the only document before the oral board, and the starting point of the interview. Know what education and experience you have listed there, and the sequence and dates of all of it. Sometimes the board will ask you to review the highlights of your experience for them; you should not have to hem and haw doing it.

2) Study the class specification and the examination announcement

Usually, the oral board has one or both of these to guide them. The qualities, characteristics or knowledges required by the position sought are stated in these documents. They offer valuable clues as to the nature of the oral interview. For example, if the job involves supervisory responsibilities, the announcement will usually indicate that knowledge of modern supervisory methods and the qualifications of the candidate as a supervisor will be tested. If so, you can expect such questions, frequently in the form of a hypothetical situation which you are expected to solve. NEVER go into an oral without knowledge of the duties and responsibilities of the job you seek.

3) Think through each qualification required

Try to visualize the kind of questions you would ask if you were a board member. How well could you answer them? Try especially to appraise your own knowledge and background in each area, *measured against the job sought*, and identify any areas in which you are weak. Be critical and realistic – do not flatter yourself.

4) Do some general reading in areas in which you feel you may be weak

For example, if the job involves supervision and your past experience has NOT, some general reading in supervisory methods and practices, particularly in the field of human relations, might be useful. Do NOT study agency procedures or detailed manuals. The oral board will be testing your understanding and capacity, not your memory.

5) Get a good night's sleep and watch your general health and mental attitude

You will want a clear head at the interview. Take care of a cold or any other minor ailment, and of course, no hangovers.

What should be done on the day of the interview?

Now comes the day of the interview itself. Give yourself plenty of time to get there. Plan to arrive somewhat ahead of the scheduled time, particularly if your appointment is in the fore part of the day. If a previous candidate fails to appear, the board might be ready for you a bit early. By early afternoon an oral board is almost invariably behind schedule if there are many candidates, and you may have to wait. Take along a book or magazine to read, or your application to review, but leave any extraneous material in the waiting room when you go in for your interview. In any event, relax and compose yourself.

The matter of dress is important. The board is forming impressions about you – from your experience, your manners, your attitude, and your appearance. Give your personal appearance careful attention. Dress your best, but not your flashiest. Choose conservative, appropriate clothing, and be sure it is immaculate. This is a business interview, and your appearance should indicate that you regard it as such. Besides, being well groomed and properly dressed will help boost your confidence.

Sooner or later, someone will call your name and escort you into the interview room. *This is it.* From here on you are on your own. It is too late for any more preparation. But remember, you asked for this opportunity to prove your fitness, and you are here because your request was granted.

What happens when you go in?

The usual sequence of events will be as follows: The clerk (who is often the board stenographer) will introduce you to the chairman of the oral board, who will introduce you to the other members of the board. Acknowledge the introductions before you sit down. Do not be surprised if you find a microphone facing you or a stenotypist sitting by. Oral interviews are usually recorded in the event of an appeal or other review.

Usually the chairman of the board will open the interview by reviewing the highlights of your education and work experience from your application – primarily for the benefit of the other members of the board, as well as to get the material into the record. Do not interrupt or comment unless there is an error or significant misinterpretation; if that is the case, do not hesitate. But do not quibble about insignificant matters. Also, he will usually ask you some question about your education, experience or your present job – partly to get you to start talking and to establish the interviewing "rapport." He may start the actual questioning, or turn it over to one of the other members. Frequently, each member undertakes the questioning on a particular area, one in which he is perhaps most competent, so you can expect each member to participate in the examination. Because time is limited, you may also expect some rather abrupt switches in the direction the questioning takes, so do not be upset by it. Normally, a board member will not pursue a single line of questioning unless he discovers a particular strength or weakness.

After each member has participated, the chairman will usually ask whether any member has any further questions, then will ask you if you have anything you wish to add. Unless you are expecting this question, it may floor you. Worse, it may start you off on an extended, extemporaneous speech. The board is not usually seeking more information. The question is principally to offer you a last opportunity to present further qualifications or to indicate that you have nothing to add. So, if you feel that a significant qualification or characteristic has been overlooked, it is proper to point it out in a sentence or so. Do not compliment the board on the thoroughness of their examination – they have been sketchy, and you know it. If you wish, merely say, "No thank you, I have nothing further to add." This is a point where you can "talk yourself out" of a good impression or fail to present an important bit of information. Remember, *you close the interview yourself.*

The chairman will then say, "That is all, Mr. _____, thank you." Do not be startled; the interview is over, and quicker than you think. Thank him, gather your belongings and take your leave. Save your sigh of relief for the other side of the door.

How to put your best foot forward

Throughout this entire process, you may feel that the board individually and collectively is trying to pierce your defenses, seek out your hidden weaknesses and embarrass and confuse you. Actually, this is not true. They are obliged to make an appraisal of your qualifications for the job you are seeking, and they want to see you in your best light. Remember, they must interview all candidates and a non-cooperative candidate may become a failure in spite of their best efforts to bring out his qualifications. Here are 15 suggestions that will help you:

1) Be natural – Keep your attitude confident, not cocky

If you are not confident that you can do the job, do not expect the board to be. Do not apologize for your weaknesses, try to bring out your strong points. The board is interested in a positive, not negative, presentation. Cockiness will antagonize any board member and make him wonder if you are covering up a weakness by a false show of strength.

2) Get comfortable, but don't lounge or sprawl

Sit erectly but not stiffly. A careless posture may lead the board to conclude that you are careless in other things, or at least that you are not impressed by the importance of the occasion. Either conclusion is natural, even if incorrect. Do not fuss with your clothing, a pencil or an ashtray. Your hands may occasionally be useful to emphasize a point; do not let them become a point of distraction.

3) Do not wisecrack or make small talk

This is a serious situation, and your attitude should show that you consider it as such. Further, the time of the board is limited – they do not want to waste it, and neither should you.

4) Do not exaggerate your experience or abilities

In the first place, from information in the application or other interviews and sources, the board may know more about you than you think. Secondly, you probably will not get away with it. An experienced board is rather adept at spotting such a situation, so do not take the chance.

5) If you know a board member, do not make a point of it, yet do not hide it

Certainly you are not fooling him, and probably not the other members of the board. Do not try to take advantage of your acquaintanceship – it will probably do you little good.

6) Do not dominate the interview

Let the board do that. They will give you the clues – do not assume that you have to do all the talking. Realize that the board has a number of questions to ask you, and do not try to take up all the interview time by showing off your extensive knowledge of the answer to the first one.

7) Be attentive

You only have 20 minutes or so, and you should keep your attention at its sharpest throughout. When a member is addressing a problem or question to you, give him your undivided attention. Address your reply principally to him, but do not exclude the other board members.

8) Do not interrupt

A board member may be stating a problem for you to analyze. He will ask you a question when the time comes. Let him state the problem, and wait for the question.

9) Make sure you understand the question

Do not try to answer until you are sure what the question is. If it is not clear, restate it in your own words or ask the board member to clarify it for you. However, do not haggle about minor elements.

10) Reply promptly but not hastily

A common entry on oral board rating sheets is "candidate responded readily," or "candidate hesitated in replies." Respond as promptly and quickly as you can, but do not jump to a hasty, ill-considered answer.

11) Do not be peremptory in your answers

A brief answer is proper – but do not fire your answer back. That is a losing game from your point of view. The board member can probably ask questions much faster than you can answer them.

12) Do not try to create the answer you think the board member wants

He is interested in what kind of mind you have and how it works – not in playing games. Furthermore, he can usually spot this practice and will actually grade you down on it.

13) Do not switch sides in your reply merely to agree with a board member

Frequently, a member will take a contrary position merely to draw you out and to see if you are willing and able to defend your point of view. Do not start a debate, yet do not surrender a good position. If a position is worth taking, it is worth defending.

14) Do not be afraid to admit an error in judgment if you are shown to be wrong

The board knows that you are forced to reply without any opportunity for careful consideration. Your answer may be demonstrably wrong. If so, admit it and get on with the interview.

15) Do not dwell at length on your present job

The opening question may relate to your present assignment. Answer the question but do not go into an extended discussion. You are being examined for a *new* job, not your present one. As a matter of fact, try to phrase ALL your answers in terms of the job for which you are being examined.

Basis of Rating

Probably you will forget most of these "do's" and "don'ts" when you walk into the oral interview room. Even remembering them all will not ensure you a passing grade. Perhaps you did not have the qualifications in the first place. But remembering them will help you to put your best foot forward, without treading on the toes of the board members.

Rumor and popular opinion to the contrary notwithstanding, an oral board wants you to make the best appearance possible. They know you are under pressure – but they also want to see how you respond to it as a guide to what your reaction would be under the pressures of the job you seek. They will be influenced by the degree of poise you display, the personal traits you show and the manner in which you respond.

ABOUT THIS BOOK

This book contains tests divided into Examination Sections. Go through each test, answering every question in the margin. At the end of each test look at the answer key and check your answers. On the ones you got wrong, look at the right answer choice and learn. Do not fill in the answers first. Do not memorize the questions and answers, but understand the answer and principles involved. On your test, the questions will likely be different from the samples. Questions are changed and new ones added. If you understand these past questions you should have success with any changes that arise. Tests may consist of several types of questions. We have additional books on each subject should more study be advisable or necessary for you. Finally, the more you study, the better prepared you will be. This book is intended to be the last thing you study before you walk into the examination room. Prior study of relevant texts is also recommended. NLC publishes some of these in our Fundamental Series. Knowledge and good sense are important factors in passing your exam. Good luck also helps. So now study this Passbook, absorb the material contained within and take that knowledge into the examination. Then do your best to pass that exam.

———

EXAMINATION SECTION

EXAMINATION SECTION
TEST 1

DIRECTIONS: Each question or incomplete statement is followed by several suggested answers or completions. Select the one that BEST answers the question or completes the statement. *PRINT THE LETTER OF THE CORRECT ANSWER IN THE SPACE AT THE RIGHT.*

1. The current trend among MOST ecologists is to consider the coastal zones of America   1.____

    A. a group of diverse, stable ecosystems whose respective managements require a variety of individual approaches
    B. systems that are unique to this continent and require an entirely different set of management techniques from other continental coast zones
    C. a group of unstable ecosystems whose already fragile balance has been destroyed by modern industrial practices
    D. a single natural ecosystem requiring integration of management techniques

2. Of the following methods for controlling industrial particulate discharge into the air, the one which has the GREATEST potential efficiency is   2.____

    A. wet scrubbing
    B. fabric filter bag house
    C. electrostatic precipitation
    D. cyclone filter

3. The process by which objects or solid materials are removed from a water supply is called   3.____

    A. straining   B. treatment
    C. screening   D. precipitating

4. All of the following are generally considered obstacles to United States air quality control operations EXCEPT   4.____

    A. high number of uncertain cause-effect relationships
    B. resistance from industrial operations
    C. little danger perceived by the public
    D. relatively small number of particulate contaminants that have been identified

5. The MOST critical step in any given industrial waste management program is the   5.____

    A. phase separation   B. preliminary investigation
    C. process modification   D. contaminant removal

6. The one of the following that is NOT an option for the control of coastal management offered by the Federal Coastal Management Program is   6.____

    A. direct state control
    B. local control subject to state review
    C. local control consistent with state standards
    D. regional control based upon state collaboration

7. The process through which gaseous contaminants are removed from the air is called   7._____

    A. desorption   B. adsorption
    C. distillation   D. precipitation

8. An automobile's catalytic converter is designed to keep all of the following contaminants   8._____
from being discharged into the air EXCEPT

    A. lead   B. carbon monoxide
    C. hydrocarbons   D. nitrogen oxides

9. Which of the following is a chemical process of waste-water treatment?   9._____

    A. Screening   B. Distillation
    C. Sedimentation   D. Coagulation

10. The stage that occurs LAST in the treatment process of sanitary sewage is   10._____

    A. sedimentation
    B. screening out solids
    C. biological oxidation
    D. filtering through grit chambers

11. The element of air quality control that can be monitored but NOT managed is   11._____

    A. regulatory standards
    B. emissions
    C. meteorology and dispersion
    D. air quality

12. Currently, the rationale behind MOST water quality control operations is   12._____

    A. public health
    B. aesthetic qualities of water resource
    C. protection of aquatic life
    D. preserving recreational capabilities of water resource

13. In the process of air quality improvement, the practice used as a precleaning process   13._____
before more efficient methods are applied is called

    A. electrostatic precipitation
    B. mechanical cleaning
    C. gas conditioning
    D. process modifications

14. Which of the following practiced methods for desaliniza-tion of water makes use of a salt-   14._____
filtering membrane?

    A. Freezing   B. Distillation
    C. Reverse osmosis   D. Electrodialysis

15. The FUNDAMENTAL criterion for managing coastal basins is the   15._____

    A. geological configuration of the basin
    B. depth of the basin
    C. ecological vitality of the system
    D. degree of water exchange or flushing rate

16. The LEAST desirable method for heating gases that are intended to be released from an air cleaning unit is by   16.____

    A. direct combustion
    B. heat exchangers
    C. indirect heating of ambient air
    D. cooling entering gases

17. Of the following stages of conventional wastewater treatment, the one that occurs FIRST is   17.____

    A. chlorination   B. sedimentation
    C. oxidation   D. discharge

18. The air quality control devices capable of removing BOTH particulate and gaseous contaminants from the air are   18.____

    A. cyclone filters   B. wet scrubbers
    C. adsorbers   D. filter baghouses

19. The process of restoration is considered acceptable by MOST ecologists if it is implemented to   19.____

    A. compensate for an operation that has been projected as being harmful
    B. correct inadvertent harm or past problems
    C. mitigate the damage in advance of a harmful practice
    D. improve the aesthetics of an environment that is near development

20. Turbidity, or ultrafine particle solids in a water supply, are PRIMARILY removed through the process of   20.____

    A. screening   B. distillation
    C. coagulation   D. oxidation

21. The object of chemical removal processes in air quality control is to   21.____

    A. convert gases to particulate matter
    B. increase the water saturation point of the air medium
    C. convert gases into innocuous chemical compounds
    D. vaporize particulate matter

22. Which of the following is NOT a practice associated with the restoration of silt-polluted coastal basins?   22.____

    A. Limiting dredging to active vegetative periods
    B. Construction of bulkheads along the shore
    C. Implementation of soil conservation practices in adjacent farmlands
    D. Diversion of runoff waters from basin

23. _____ standards are applied to municipal water control operations to specify the MAXIMUM concentration of certain constituents of a given water supply,   23.____

    A. Procedural   B. Performance
    C. Investigation   D. Design

24. Which of the following is NOT among the most effective methods for the prevention of aquifer contamination?

    24.____

    A. Industrial zoning
    B. Strict chemical storage rules
    C. Trenching
    D. Watershed protection

25. Of the following, the chemical process that is NOT considered a control mechanism for air quality is

    25.____

    A. masking   B. particulate conversion
    C. reduction   D. oxidation

————

KEY (CORRECT ANSWERS)

1.	D		11.	C
2.	C		12.	C
3.	C		13.	B
4.	C		14.	C
5.	B		15.	D
6.	D		16.	A
7.	B		17.	B
8.	A		18.	B
9.	D		19.	B
10.	C		20.	C

21.	A
22.	A
23.	B
24.	C
25.	A

————

TEST 2

DIRECTIONS: Each question or incomplete statement is followed by several suggested answers or completions. Select the one that BEST answers the question or completes the statement. *PRINT THE LETTER OF THE CORRECT ANSWER IN THE SPACE AT THE RIGHT.*

1. The term for the process that removes algae or turbidity from a water supply during the water treatment process is

    A. screening
    B. straining
    C. treatment
    D. discharge

1.____

2. The method for treating groundwater contamination MOST often used for drinking water supplies is _____ treatment.

    A. chemical
    B. carbon
    C. aerobic biological
    D. ozonation/radiation

2.____

3. Which of the following is NOT one of the primary factors determining the operation of coastal basin management?

    A. Circulation type
    B. Climate
    C. Geology
    D. Depth

3.____

4. All of the following are practical methods for limiting the discharge of sulfur oxides into the air EXCEPT

    A. desulfurization of oil
    B. limiting coal use to low-sulfur varieties
    C. removal of sulfur from industrial water supplies
    D. removal of sulfur from coal

4.____

5. The one of the following that is NOT a practice associated with the construction of spoil islands that will protect marina sites in coastal waters is

    A. vegetation with both upland plants and marsh grasses
    B. avoidance of existing vital areas
    C. constructing elliptical islands parallel to water flow
    D. use of fine soil materials in construction

5.____

6. The FIRST step in any water quality control procedure is

    A. determination of the plant site
    B. compilation of data needed to reach sound decisions about objectives
    C. imposing immediate short-term controls on water quality
    D. establishment of design standards for plant operations

6.____

7. Of the following methods for controlling industrial particulate discharge into the air, the one that makes use of gravitational forces is

    A. wet scrubbing
    B. fabric filter bag house
    C. electrostatic precipitation
    D. cyclone filter

7.____

8. An example of a physical process of wastewater treatment is   8.____

    A. coagulation   B. distillation
    C. ion exchange   D. pH adjustment

9. The type of marine environment that is considered to be MOST in need of management   9.____
is the

    A. lagoon   B. bay
    C. ocean   D. tidal river

10. Of the practiced methods for desalinization of water, the MOST widely used in the United   10.____
States is

    A. freezing   B. distillation
    C. reverse osmosis   D. electrodialysis

11. Each of the following is a noncrystalline adsorbent used to remove contaminants from   11.____
the air EXCEPT

    A. metallic oxides   B. activated carbon
    C. silica gel   D. D, activated alumina

12. The guiding practice of a shorelands management operation is   12.____

    A. excavating drainage canals
    B. clearing vegetation
    C. maintaining natural drainage and stream flow
    D. covering land with impervious surfaces

13. In water treatment, the mixing process during which particles form into aggregate   13.____
masses that settle out is called

    A. osmosis   B. flocculation
    C. straining   D. oxidation

14. The type of standards applied to municipal water control operations that specify the   14.____
required characteristics of a given water supply are _____ standards.

    A. design   B. performance
    C. procedural   D. investigation

15. _____ standards are applied to municipal water control operations that define the   15.____
approaches and methods followed in water quality control activities.

    A. Procedural   B. Design
    C. Investigation   D. Performance

16. Marsh-grass plantings are widely used near coastal waters for all of the following pur-   16.____
poses EXCEPT

    A. stabilizing dredge spoil
    B. creation of marshes
    C. revitalization of microorganisms
    D. creation of alternative bulkheads

17. Which of the following has NOT been widely attempted as a method for the control of automotive emissions?   17.____

    A. Reduction of automobile traffic in urban areas
    B. Altering the composition of motor fuels
    C. Filtering or converting devices for emissions
    D. Modification of the conventional engine

18. The guiding factor for what is an acceptable MINIMUM flow into coastal ecosystems is the   18.____

    A. sedimentation of inlet basin
    B. strength of tidal backflow
    C. critical survival point for microorganisms
    D. dry-season low flows under natural conditions

19. In preparing water that is to be considered drinkable, the PRIMARY method for odor prevention is   19.____

    A. chlorine-ammonia treatment
    B. fluoridation
    C. flocculation
    D. filtration

20. The MOST effective method for containing a contaminant leakage plume that has deeply penetrated an underground water source is   20.____

    A. trenching
    B. installing a clay barrier
    C. well pumping
    D. chemical or biological treatment

21. The ULTIMATE goal of the 1972 Amendment to the Water Pollution Control Act was   21.____

    A. enforceable standards limiting industrial waste disposal practices in United States waters
    B. total elimination of the discharge of pollutants into navigable United States waters
    C. banning of the production and marketing of harmful water pollutants
    D. elimination of water pollutants categorized as *most dangerous* by the Environmental Protection Agency

22. The process by which contaminant chemicals are removed during the water treatment process is called   22.____

    A. screening   B. sedimentation
    C. straining   D. treatment

23. All of the following are aspects of major concern in the protection of coastal basins EXCEPT   23.____

    A. changes in circulation caused by alteration of basin configuration
    B. degradation of ecological condition of basin and its margins
    C. loss of ecologically vital areas
    D. salinity of basin waters

24. The process of lime coagulation is used to remove _____ from a water supply.   24.____

    A. phosphates   B. lead
    C. nitrates   D. iron

25. Of the following, the LEAST effective method for controlling the effect of automotive   25.____
emissions has been

    A. parking restrictions in urban areas
    B. carpooling incentives
    C. modification of liquid fuels
    D. toll bridges and highways

———

KEY (CORRECT ANSWERS)

1.	B		11.	A
2.	B		12.	C
3.	B		13.	B
4.	C		14.	A
5.	D		15.	A
6.	B		16.	C
7.	D		17.	D
8.	B		18.	D
9.	A		19.	A
10.	B		20.	C

21.	B
22.	D
23.	D
24.	A
25.	C

———

EXAMINATION SECTION
TEST 1

DIRECTIONS: Each question or incomplete statement is followed by several suggested answers or completions. Select the one that BEST answers the question or completes the statement. *PRINT THE LETTER OF THE CORRECT ANSWER IN THE SPACE AT THE RIGHT.*

1. The MOST efficient devices to measure the gaseous pollutant content of an air sample are   1.____

    A. cyclones   B. filters
    C. bubblers   D. settling chambers

2. The source MOST likely to cause high concentrations of toxic metals associated with nonpoint source water pollution is   2.____

    A. construction   B. highway de-icing
    C. on-site sewage disposal   D. urban storm runoff

3. In the United States, the required landfill space per person each year is GENERALLY   3.____

    A. ten cubic feet   B. one cubic yard
    C. one cubic acre   D. ten square feet

4. The easiest and most effective method for controlling air pollution is   4.____

    A. source correction   B. treatment
    C. collection   D. dispersion

5. The MOST serious source of air pollution associated with the automobile is the   5.____

    A. fuel tank   B. carburetor
    C. crankcase   D. exhaust

6. Which of the following practices or devices is considered to be a collection or treatment control for urban storm-water runoff?   6.____

    A. Anti-littering laws   B. Street cleaning
    C. Floodplain zoning   D. Detention systems

7. The increasing trend in solid waste disposal in the United States is toward the practice of   7.____

    A. incineration
    B. ocean dumping
    C. sanitary landfill
    D. recycling/resource reclamation

8. The MOST widely practiced method for cooling air pollutants before they reach control equipment is   8.____

    A. dilution   B. settling
    C. heat exchange coils   D. quenching

9. Which of the following is NOT a factor of required knowledge for solving an upgrade problem in wastewater treatment plants?   9.____

A. Staffing pattern
B. Normal operational and maintenance procedures
C. Daily peak flow rates
D. Condition of process hardware

10. The category of solid waste that constitutes the GREATEST volume percentage in the United States is   10.____

    A. residential   B. bulky wastes
    C. commercial   D. industrial

11. In current practice, the SIMPLEST test for ozone content of an air sample measures the air's reaction with   11.____

    A. metals with high lead content
    B. rubber
    C. organics
    D. copper

12. High concentrations of acid pollutants associated with nonpoint source water pollution are MOST likely to be contributed by   12.____

    A. non-coal mining   B. air pollution fallout
    C. agriculture   D. forestry

13. Which of the following methods is used by analysts to measure the concentration of hydrocarbons in an air supply?   13.____

    A. Chemical luminescence   B. Flame ionization
    C. Infrared spectrometry   D. High-volume sampling

14. Environmental engineers generally consider _____ to be the BEST cover material for sanitary landfill sites.   14.____

    A. sandy loam   B. clay
    C. gravel   D. silt

15. Deceleration of an automobile is most likely to cause the HIGHEST relative increase in the amount of   15.____

    A. hydrocarbons   B. carbon monoxide
    C. nitrogen oxides   D. lead

16. The _____method for sanitary landfilling involves the distribution of waste into discrete *cells*.   16.____

    A. slope   B. area   C. ramp   D. trench

17. A DISADVANTAGE associated with the use of controlled burning for solid waste disposal is   17.____

    A. consumption of a large amount of resources
    B. lingering contamination of burn site
    C. increased transport costs
    D. large land area required

18. Each of the following is a primary factor in the determination of the area required for a sanitary landfill site EXCEPT   18.____

    A. percent reduction, by compaction, of on-site refuse volume
    B. amount of cover material required
    C. total projected amount of refuse to be delivered
    D. average density of refuse delivered to landfill

19. The method of solid waste disposal that currently involves the GREATEST costs in capital investment is   19.____

    A. incineration
    C. landfilling
    B. ocean dumping
    D. composting

20. The substance normally used in filters to detect the presence of sulfur dioxide in an air sample is   20.____

    A. microorganisms
    C. lead peroxide
    B. sulfur
    D. carbon

21. Which of the following is NOT a quality parameter of concern in the activated carbon treatment of wastewater?   21.____

    A. Heavy metals
    C. Trace organics
    B. Suspended solids
    D. Dissolved oxygen

22. The problem that presents the GREATEST potential hazard to landfill sites is   22.____

    A. pests
    C. gas
    B. water pollution
    D. decomposition

23. The MOST serious problem associated with the investigative practice of industrial stack sampling is   23.____

    A. control of potentially great capital expense
    B. risk of obtaining an unrepresentative sample
    C. safety risks for analysts
    D. skewing of sample readings by heat concentrations

24. The MOST common method for disinfection in wastewater treatment plants is   24.____

    A. ozone treatment
    B. ultraviolet light exposure
    C. chlorination
    D. introduction of bromine chloride

25. Of the following categories for the pollution control of urban stormwater runoff, _____ controls are considered to be the MOST effective and inexpensive.   25.____

    A. planning
    C. treatment
    B. accumulation
    D. collection

KEY (CORRECT ANSWERS)

1.	C	11.	B
2.	D	12.	A
3.	B	13.	B
4.	A	14.	A
5.	D	15.	A
6.	D	16.	B
7.	D	17.	C
8.	C	18.	C
9.	C	19.	D
10.	D	20.	C

21.	A
22.	B
23.	B
24.	C
25.	A

TEST 2

DIRECTIONS: Each question or incomplete statement is followed by several suggested answers or completions. Select the one that BEST answers the question or completes the statement. *PRINT THE LETTER OF THE CORRECT ANSWER IN THE SPACE AT THE RIGHT.*

1. _____% of solid waste in the United States is considered compostible.   1.____

   A. 5-10   B. 20-30   C. 50-75   D. 80-85

2. Which of the following is NOT considered to be a factor affecting the level of organic   2.____
   decomposition in sanitary landfills?

   A. Moisture   B. Surface area of fill
   C. Temperature   D. Depth of fill

3. The SIMPLEST and MOST widely used device for controlling the particulate content of   3.____
   an air supply is the

   A. settling chamber   B. adsorber
   C. wet collector   D. bubbler

4. The agricultural practice MOST likely to contribute high levels of total dissolved solids to   4.____
   nonpoint source water pollution is

   A. animal production
   B. irrigated crop production
   C. pasturing and rangeland
   D. non-irrigated crop production

5. Pathogenic bacteria in wastewater supplies are likely to be produced by each of the fol-   5.____
   lowing EXCEPT

   A. construction operations
   B. food processing industries
   C. pharmaceutical manufacturing
   D. tanneries

6. The substance MOST often used to remove sulfur from discharged flue gases is   6.____

   A. copper   B. lime   C. water   D. acid

7. In controlling automotive emissions, an activated carbon canister is used to store emis-   7.____
   sions from the

   A. manifold   B. fuel tank
   C. crankcase   D. exhaust

8. Which of the following is NOT a disadvantage associated with the use of sanitary landfill   8.____
   sites for solid waste disposal?

   A. High collection costs
   B. Jurisdiction entanglements
   C. Large amount of land required
   D. Difficulties presented by seasonal changes

9. The Ringelmann scale is a device used to measure the _____ of an air sample.   9._____

    A. smoke density   B. odor
    C. temperature   D. gaseous pollutant content

10. High-volume sampling is a method for detecting   10._____

    A. ozone   B. oxidant
    C. particulate   D. sulfur dioxide

11. An example of air pollution abatement, as opposed to source control, is   11._____

    A. change of raw material   B. modification of process
    C. equipment modifications   D. stack dispersion

12. *Pollutant loading* is a term that defines the   12._____

    A. collection of pollutants for treatment in a control exercise
    B. quantity of pollution detached and transported into surface watercourses
    C. saturation point of any environment in terms of its pollutant capacity
    D. process of contamination, by an industrial source, of the ambient air

13. Each of the following is an advantage associated with the controlled burning of solid   13._____
wastes EXCEPT

    A. land can be returned to immediate use
    B. sites are longer-lasting
    C. reduced amount of required land
    D. relatively easy collection and transport of materials

14. The device capable of removing the smallest particle from an air supply is the   14._____

    A. electrostatic precipitator
    B. settling chamber
    C. bag filter
    D. wet collector

15. High concentrations of suspended solids associated with nonpoint source water pollution   15._____
are MOST likely contributed by

    A. urban storm runoff
    B. construction
    C. air pollution fallout
    D. non-irrigated crop production

16. Which of the following is NOT one of the primary steps involved in the control of gaseous   16._____
air pollutants?

    A. Removal of pollutant from emissions
    B. Change in process producing pollutant
    C. Dispersion of the pollutant
    D. Chemical conversion of the pollutant

17. To control automotive air pollution, the process of recycling blow-by gases is a method   17._____
for controlling emissions from the

    A. fuel tank   B. exhaust
    C. carburetor   D. crankcase

18. In testing a water supply for the presence of coliform bacteria, the survey method MOST   18._____
likely to be used is

    A. oxygen demand   B. dissolved oxygen
    C. total dissolved solids   D. suspended solids

19. In measuring the constituency of a given air supply, analysts use the process of infrared   19._____
spectrometry to determine concentrations of

    A. oxidants   B. carbon monoxide
    C. sulfur dioxide   D. particulates

20. Which of the following is NOT one of the primary factors affecting the choice of pollution   20._____
control methods for urban stormwater runoff?

    A. Specific constituents of runoff
    B. Type of sewage system
    C. Status of area development
    D. Method of land use

21. A disadvantage associated with the use of sanitary landfill sites for solid waste disposal   21._____
is

    A. high personnel and plant costs
    B. weakened accomodation of peak quantities
    C. potential for groundwater pollution
    D. difficulty with unusual, bulky materials

22. The MOST serious problem in air pollution is presented by   22._____

    A. cooling of pollutants   B. treatment of pollutants
    C. collection of pollutants   D. source modifications

23. Of the following practices or devices, the one considered to be an accumulation control   23._____
for urban stormwater runoff is

    A. automobile inspection   B. street cleaning
    C. floodplain zoning   D. catch basins

24. _____ is used to survey an air sample for the presence of sulfur dioxide.   24._____

    A. Liquid medium   B. Colorimetry
    C. High-volume sampling   D. Flame ionization

25. Acceleration of an automobile is most likely to cause the HIGHEST relative increase in   25._____
the amount of

    A. hydrocarbons   B. carbon monoxide
    C. nitrogen oxides   D. lead

KEY (CORRECT ANSWERS)

1.	D	11.	D
2.	B	12.	B
3.	A	13.	D
4.	B	14.	A
5.	A	15.	B
6.	B	16.	C
7.	B	17.	D
8.	A	18.	A
9.	A	19.	B
10.	C	20.	A

21.	C
22.	C
23.	B
24.	B
25.	C

EXAMINATION SECTION
TEST 1

DIRECTIONS: Each question or incomplete statement is followed by several suggested answers or completions. Select the one that BEST answers the question or completes the statement. *PRINT THE LETTER OF THE CORRECT ANSWER IN THE SPACE AT THE RIGHT.*

1. Which of the following types of parameters is NOT generally considered to be one of the primary factors in defining environmental quality?

    A. Physical   B. Meteorological
    C. Biological   D. Chemical

1.____

2. All of the following resources are listed in the National Wildlife Federation's annual Environmental Quality Index EXCEPT

    A. timber   B. human population
    C. minerals   D. living space

2.____

3. In dollars, the costs of low air quality in the United States are GREATEST in relation to

    A. human health   B. materials
    C. vegetation   D. residential property

3.____

4. Evaluations of soil quality are MOST commonly expressed in terms of

    A. chemical contamination
    B. erodibility
    C. mineral constituency
    D. use of soluble nitrogen forms

4.____

5. Of the methods for water quality measurement below, which does NOT measure the effects of a given constituent?

    A. Threshold odor tests
    B. Bioassays of live fish
    C. Tests for chromium concentration
    D. Tests for *hardness*

5.____

6. Environmental quality indices are MOST successfully used for

    A. resource allocation   B. public information
    C. scientific research   D. enforcement of standards

6.____

7. In conducting water quality assessments intended to reveal the incidence of pathogens, _____ is MOST often the focus.

    A. nonpathogenic bacteria   B. ammonia
    C. microscopic plants   D. pathogens

7.____

8. Each of the following is a primary use of air quality data by state and local agencies EXCEPT

8.____

A. determination of compliance with standards
B. reporting daily quality levels to the public
C. determination of critical episodes requiring emer-gency measures
D. enacting quality legislation

9. Of the following units for evaluating the radioactivity of an environment, _____ is a mea-sure of the activity of radioactive materials.   9.____

A. rad
C. curie

B. dose equivalent
D. roentgen

10. The one of the following that is NOT a factor in calculat-ing the average soil loss for a given crop rotation is   10.____

A. temperature
C. rainfall

B. erosion control practice
D. length of slope

11. Which of the following devices for assessing the quality of a radioactive environment offers the LEAST accurate quantitative measurements?   11.____

A. Counter
C. Magnetic filter

B. Ionization chamber
D. Photographic film

12. Solid-media water quality assessments that produce a green substance on the medium indicate   12.____

A. algae
C. pathogens

B. coliform bacteria
D. chlorine

13. The MOST important factor in determining the quality of a water resource is the   13.____

A. purpose for which the water is being considered
B. flow capacity of the resource
C. chemical purity of the water
D. biotic potential of the resource

14. According to the National Wildlife Federation's annual Environmental Quality Index, of the United States' resources, _____ is in the BEST relative condition.   14.____

A. timber   B. air   C. water   D. soil

15. Which of the following is NOT usually a component of quality of life surveys conducted in urban environments?   15.____

A. Political
C. Ecological

B. Economic
D. Health and education

16. Approximately _____% of the earth's water supply is drinkable.   16.____

A. .5   B. 1-3   C. 3-5   D. 5-10

17. A land-use quality index that measures the number of acres lost or gained to wildlife is known as a(n)_____ index.   17.____

A. encroachment
C. habitat change

B. overlap
D. urban green

18. Which of the following methods of water quality evaluation is considered a last resort by analysts?   18.____

    A. Measurement of factors associated with a given constituent
    B. Measuring the effects of constituents
    C. Qualitative descriptions
    D. Direct measurement of constituent concentrations

19. _____ is NOT one of the primary impact standards by which air quality is evaluated.   19.____

    A. Esthetic   B. Meteorological
    C. Health   D. Economic

20. The expression of pesticide injury to plants is a function of each of the following EXCEPT   20.____

    A. chemical properties of the pesticide
    B. sorptive ability of soil
    C. soil erodibility
    D. climatic conditions

21. Of the following, experts have developed the LEAST definitive quality index so far for   21.____

    A. total environment   B. air
    C. solid waste   D. water

22. Of the methods for water quality measurement below, which is an example of DIRECT measurement and reportage of a given concentration?   22.____

    A. Determination of the iron content of drinking water
    B. Determining water *hardness*
    C. Measuring alkalinity
    D. Turbidity analysis

23. In order to determine the quality of a solid waste disposal management system, each of the following charac-teristics of solid waste must be measured EXCEPT   23.____

    A. particle size   B. density
    C. chemical makeup   D. waste source

24. _____ is a measure of absorbed radiation dosage.   24.____

    A. Rad   B. Dose equivalent
    C. Roentgen   D. Curie

25. According to the National Wildlife Federation, of the resources given below, _____ has the GREATEST relativeimportance to human life.   25.____

    A. air   B. wildlife   C. soil   D. water

KEY (CORRECT ANSWERS)

1.	B		11.	D
2.	B		12.	B
3.	A		13.	A
4.	D		14.	D
5.	C		15.	C
6.	B		16.	A
7.	C		17.	C
8.	D		18.	C
9.	C		19.	B
10.	A		20.	C

21.	A
22.	A
23.	D
24.	A
25.	C

TEST 2

DIRECTIONS: Each question or incomplete statement is followed by several suggested answers or completions. Select the one that BEST answers the question or completes the statement. *PRINT THE LETTER OF THE CORRECT ANSWER IN THE SPACE AT THE RIGHT.*

1. The appearance of a purple culture in the Gram-stain water quality assessment indicates a _____ result for _____.   1.____

    A. positive; microscopic plants
    B. negative; coliforms
    C. positive; blue-green algae
    D. negative; pathogens

2. The constituent LEAST likely to be measured by an Air Quality Index is   2.____

    A. hydrocarbon   B. sulfur dioxide
    C. particulate   D. carbon monoxide

3. A land-use quality index that is limited to assessing *man-made* environments is known as a(n) _____ index.   3.____

    A. encroachment   B. overlap
    C. habitat change   D. urban green

4. Which of the following is NOT an example of a quantitative water quality measurement based on an arbitrary scale?   4.____

    A. Suspended solids   B. Volatile solids
    C. Acidity   D. Color

5. The degree to which an environment can be considered *natural* is measured PRIMARILY in terms of   5.____

    A. the total species diversity of the environment
    B. the type of management imposed on the environment
    C. the degree to which ecological succession is allowed to take place
    D. its current station in the process of ecological succession

6. The ability of a soil resource to retain nitrogen is a function of each of the following EXCEPT   6.____

    A. altitude   B. aeration
    C. soil texture   D. temperature

7. The basis for judging whether a water resource is suitable for the uses under consideration is determined by   7.____

    A. absolute standards of purity and biotic potential that are established locally
    B. comparison of uses with projected capacity of the resource
    C. consensus of the population to be served by the resource
    D. comparison of data with published criteria concerning the purpose of the resource

8. For the sake of simplicity and comprehensiveness, MOST of the Environmental Protection Agency's quality reports take the form of   8.____

    A. anecdotal reports   B. bar graphs and charts
    C. raw data   D. time series plots

9. In measuring the ecological quality of an environment, which of the following categories   9.____
of vegetation properties is NOT used as an indicator?

    A. Elemental composition   B. Morphology
    C. Specific growth rates   D. Species presence

10. Of the following devices for assessing the quality of a radioactive environment, the one   10.____
designed to note the movement of single particles through a defined volume is

    A. photographic film   B. ionization chamber
    C. magnetic filter   D. counter

11. Of the methods for water quality measurement below, which is an example of a qualita-   11.____
tive description?

    A. Microbiological content
    B. Floating matter and debris
    C. Turbidity
    D. Mercury concentration limits

12. According to the National Wildlife Federation's annual Environmental Quality Index, of   12.____
the United States' resources, _____ is in the WORST relative condition.

    A. wildlife   B. air   C. water   D. soil

13. Which of the following factors is NOT usually included in measurements of the effects of   13.____
environmental noise on humans?

    A. Frequency spectrum
    B. Time variations of frequency and sound level
    C. Noise source
    D. Overall sound level

14. Most analysts agree that an accurate, readable index measuring the quality of a total   14.____
environment would have to include _____ factors.

    A. fewer than thirty
    B. between forty and seventy
    C. no more than ten
    D. over 100

15. A soil quality index intended for measuring pesticide residue must be a function of each   15.____
of the following variables EXCEPT

    A. irrigation practices   B. pesticide
    C. crop   D. climate

16. The method of water quality measurement considered by analysts to be the quickest and   16.____
most accurate is

A. measurement of factors associated with a given constituent
B. qualitative descriptions
C. direct measurement of constituent concentrations
D. measurement of the effects of a given constituent

17. A land-use quality index that measures the proportion of developed to undeveloped land   17.____
is known as a(n) _____ index.

    A. encroachment   B. overlap
    C. habitat change   D. urban green

18. Which of the following is NOT among the basic uses for environmental quality indices?   18.____

    A. Public information
    B. Ranking of industries by quality level
    C. Ranking of locations by quality level
    D. Trend analysis

19. The baseline alkalinity concentration criteria for a freshwater resource's ability to support   19.____
aquatic life is generally considered to be _____milligrams per liter.

    A. no more than 10   B. between 5 and 50
    C. between 0 and 15   D. no less than 20

20. In evaluating the quality of a soil resource, the MOST difficult aspect to determine accu-   20.____
rately is

    A. aeration
    B. the form taken by nitrates
    C. moisture content
    D. total nitrogen content

21. All of the following are main classes of air quality measurements EXCEPT   21.____

    A. ambient air quality   B. meteorological
    C. radiological   D. emissions

22. _____is MOST likely to cause taste and odor problems in a surface water supply.   22.____

    A. Coliform bacteria   B. Fluoride
    C. Chlorine   D. Algae

23. Of the methods for air quality measurement given below, which is used to detect and   23.____
measure the incidence of carbon monoxide?

    A. Infrared spectrometry   B. Chemical luminescence
    C. Flame ionization   D. High-volume sampling

24. Of the methods for water quality measurement below, the one which is NOT an example   24.____
of measuring factors associated with a given constituent is

    A. biochemical oxygen demand
    B. suspended solids measurement
    C. use of total organic carbon
    D. *indicator organism* tests

25. According to the National Wildlife Federation, of the resources below, _____ has the   25._____
    LEAST relative importance to human life.

    A. air   B. wildlife
    C. minerals   D. living space

———

KEY (CORRECT ANSWERS)

1.	B		11.	B
2.	A		12.	B
3.	A		13.	C
4.	B		14.	D
5.	C		15.	A
6.	A		16.	A
7.	D		17.	D
8.	B		18.	B
9.	C		19.	D
10.	D		20.	B

21.	C
22.	D
23.	A
24.	B
25.	B

———

EXAMINATION SECTION
TEST 1

DIRECTIONS: Each question or incomplete statement is followed by several suggested answers or completions. Select the one that BEST answers the question or completes the statement. *PRINT THE LETTER OF THE CORRECT ANSWER IN THE SPACE AT THE RIGHT.*

1. Which of the following natural resources is classified as inexhaustible/immutable, or incapable of much change or alteration through human activity?   1____

    A. Agricultural products
    B. Atomic energy
    C. Waterpower of flowing streams
    D. Mineral resources

2. Each of the following practices is a current method for maintaining the utility of cattle grazing rangeland EXCEPT   2____

    A. manipulating stock herds
    B. reseeding
    C. firing
    D. maintaining constant grazing pressure

3. The one of the following considered to be an ADVANTAGE of monocultural forest harvesting is   3____

    A. superior wood quality
    B. makes use of built-in ecological balancing mechanisms
    C. allows nurturing of shade-intolerant species
    D. decreased susceptibility to fires

4. The type of soil that is BEST able to hold water is   4____

    A. silt
    C. silty clay
    B. sandy clay
    D. loam

5. The practice of *chipping, or* breaking the forest harvest down into smaller particles that can be compressed into useful products, can INCREASE the forest yield by _____ %.   5____

    A. 25   B. 50   C. 100   D. 200

6. The _____ industry generates the MOST revenue in the United States.   6____

    A. steel
    C. textiles
    B. cattle
    D. automobile

7. Which of the following is NOT considered to be a guiding principle in the current model for conserving natural resources?   7____

    A. Balancing individual privilege with individual responsibility
    B. Ultimate government control of conservation efforts
    C. Concentrated, singular use of particular resources
    D. Frequent inventory and projection of resource use

8. One of soil's macronutrients is   8____

    A. cobalt   B. calcium   C. zinc   D. copper

9. Food production in the United States is currently hindered by all of the following factors   9____
EXCEPT the

    A. loss of farmland to land development
    B. gradually increasing average temperatures
    C. huge fossil fuel input requirement for production
    D. transfer of water to urban populations

10. The bark of trees, long discarded as useless by loggers, has proven to be a useful   10____
resource for all of the following purposes EXCEPT

    A. medical uses
    B. construction of building frames
    C. production of chemicals for tanning leather
    D. oil-well drilling compounds

11. Of the following, the one that is NOT generally considered to be an advantage associ-   11____
ated with the use of organic fertilizers is

    A. increased rate of water release
    B. prevention of leaching
    C. improved soil structure
    D. maximum aeration of root zone

12. APPROXIMATELY _____ percent of the earth's freshwater supply is underground.   12____

    A. 30   B. 50   C. 75   D. 95

13. Which of the following is NOT generally considered to be part of the ocean's contribution   13____
as a natural resource?
A

    A. highway for international transport
    B. replenisher of oxygen supply through algeal photosynthesis
    C. major source of important vitamins in the human diet
    D. major source of important proteins in the human diet

14. The natural resource GENERALLY considered to be inexhaustible, but whose quality can   14____
be impaired by misuse, is

    A. rangeland   B. marine fish and mammals
    C. static mineral resources   D. solar energy

15. The one of the following resources that can be converted into methane gas by high-pres-   15____
sure steam heating is

    A. high-sulfur coal
    B. solid animal wastes
    C. petroleum
    D. human garbage and solid wastes

16. Given the current methods of using fossil fuels, the LEAST defensible (most wasteful), according to scientists, is   16____

    A. synthetic or bacterial food production
    B. heating
    C. petrochemicals
    D. synthetic polymers

17. The BEST way to restore soil fertility is by   17____

    A. organic fertilizers   B. inorganic fertilizers
    C. crop rotation   D. strip cropping

18. The MINIMUM amount of time that toxic material will remain in a given groundwater supply is generally considered to be _____ years.   18____

    A. 10   B. 30   C. 200   D. 1,000

19. What is considered to be the MOST influential factor governing the occurrence and behavior of aquatic life?   19____

    A. Availability of food   B. Availability of sunlight
    C. Availability of oxygen   D. Temperature

20. Which of the following has NOT proven to be a consequence involved in the use of solar energy?   20____

    A. Toxicity of working fluids
    B. Decrease in photosynthetic rates of surrounding flora
    C. Climatic change
    D. Marine pollution

21. More than 50% of the coal that has ever been mined from the earth has been extracted in the last years.   21____

    A. 100   B. 50   C. 25   D. 10

22. The natural resource classified as exhaustible but renewable, meaning that its permanence is dependent on how it is used by humans, is   22____

    A. fossil fuels   B. wildlife species
    C. solar energy   D. soil

23. The one of the following that is NOT a limiting power held by the International Whaling Commission over commercial whalers is   23____

    A. protecting certain species
    B. deciding minimum length for permissible kill
    C. protecting breeding grounds
    D. protecting calves and nursing cows

24. Which of the following is generally accepted as the MOST promising solution to the
increasing worldwide food shortage?

    24____

  A. Development of more effective fertilizers
  B. Vigorous human population control
  C. More efficient pest control
  D. Decreased reliance on meat as a food source

25. The contaminants PRIMARILY responsible for the depletion of the earth's atmospheric
ozone are

    25____

  A. carbon monoxide   B. chlorinated fluorocarbons
  C. dioxins   D. steam

KEY (CORRECT ANSWERS)

1. B		11. A
2. D		12. D
3. C		13. C
4. B		14. D
5. D		15. A
6. B		16. B
7. C		17. A
8. B		18. C
9. B		19. D
10. B		20. B

21. C
22. D
23. C
24. B
25. B

TEST 2

DIRECTIONS: Each question or incomplete statement is followed by several suggested answers or completions. Select the one that BEST answers the question or completes the statement. *PRINT THE LETTER OF THE CORRECT ANSWER IN THE SPACE AT THE RIGHT.*

1. Which of the following is currently the MOST promising method for the management of the earth's wildlife resources?

    A. Introduction of exotics
    C. Predator control
    B. B. Habitat development
    D. Game laws

    1____

2. The element of American society that is MOST responsible for consuming the largest share of energy resources is

    A. industry
    C. transportation
    B. home construction
    D. recreation

    2____

3. Of all the water drawn and transported for irrigation purposes in the United States, APPROXIMATELY _____ percent is eventually absorbed by the root systems of crops.

    A. 10   B. 25   C. 50   D. 75

    3____

4. The APPROXIMATE rate at which the Mississippi River currently carries topsoil into the Gulf of Mexico is _____ tons per _____.

    A. thirty; minute
    C. fifteen; second
    B. one hundred; minute
    D. fifty; hour

    4____

5. According to current projections, it will be approximately _____ years before the world's fossil fuel resources are completely exhausted, given current methods of use.

    A. thirty-five
    C. seventy-five
    B. fifty
    D. one hundred

    5____

6. Each of the following is considered to be a disadvantage to monocultural systems for forest harvesting EXCEPT

    A. long harvesting rotations
    B. inefficiency in growing and harvesting large crops
    C. runoff from intensive chemical use
    D. creation of oversimplified ecosystems

    6____

7. _____ is considered to be among soil's micronutrients.

    A. Manganese
    C. Potassium
    B. Nitrate
    D. Calcium

    7____

8. In relation to the population growth of the United States, what is the increase in per capita rate energy consumption? It is increasing at about _____ rate of population growth.

    A. half the
    C. twice the
    B. the same
    D. five times the

    8____

9. Which of the following is NOT considered to be a disadvantage associated with the dam-   9____
ming of flowing streams and rivers?

   A.   Decreased energy potential
   B.   Increased flooding
   C.   Sedimentation of reservoirs
   D.   Complications with the irrigating process

10. Given the topography of most United States farmland, the one of the following which has   10____
NOT proven an efficient method for the control of soil erosion by water is

   A.   contour farming   B.   gully reclamation
   C.   terracing   D.   planting shelterbelts

11. Of the following natural resources, the one classified as a consumptively used resource,   11____
or one whose eventual exhaustion is CERTAIN given current use patterns, is

   A.   gem minerals   B.   freshwater fish
   C.   stationary water sources   D.   natural gas

12. In forestry, a sustained-yield harvest program, one that produces a moderate crop that   12____
can be harvested year after year, is called

   A.   silvicultural   B.   clear-cutting
   C.   agricultural   D.   monocultural

13. Approximately _____ tons of soil are washed away ANNUALLY from the United States.   13____

   A.   fourteen million   B.   fifty-five million
   C.   one billion   D.   three billion

14. Each of the following is considered to be a disadvantage associated with *channelization*,   14____
or the artificial widening of rivers and streams, EXCEPT

   A.   loss of hardwood timber
   B.   loss of wildlife habitat
   C.   lowering of water table
   D.   increased flood risk

15. The MOST defensible (least wasteful) use of aquifer water, according to most current sci-   15____
entists, is to

   A.   irrigate monocultural crop systems
   B.   relieve drought
   C.   provide for industrial cleaning processes
   D.   fill existing reservoirs

16. Given the current methods of using fossil fuels, the MOST defensible (least wasteful)   16____
one, according to scientists, is

   A.   essential liquid fuels   B.   heating
   C.   industrial purposes   D.   electricity

17. The annual allotment of acres of _____ rangeland per head is considered to be universally standard for a single cattle animal's grazing.   17____

    A. two   B. four   C. eight   D. twelve

18. APPROXIMATELY _____ percent of the extracted forest product in the United States is used for lumber.   18____

    A. 30   B. 50   C. 70   D. 95

19. _____ is NOT considered to be an influential factor in the depletion of American soil nutrients.   19____

    A. Cropping   B. Erosion
    C. Pesticide use   D. Fertilization

20. Which of the following is NOT considered to be a factor contributing to the decline of our freshwater fish resources?   20____

    A. Decreasing habitat temperatures
    B. Toxic industrial waste
    C. Oxygen depletion
    D. Siltation

21. Of the following uses of a metallic natural resource, the one which is NOT generally considered to be consumptive or exhausting is   21____

    A. zinc in galvanized iron
    B. tin in toothpaste tubes
    C. aluminum in cans and containers
    D. lead in gasoline

22. Each of the following is an effect of oil pollution on marine ecosystems EXCEPT   22____

    A. introduction of carcinogens into food chain
    B. acceleration of photosynthetic rates
    C. concentration of chlorinated hydrocarbons
    D. immediate mortality of marine animals

23. The forestry practice of *clear-cutting* is defensively used in the   23____

    A. old-growth firs of the Pacific Northwest
    B. oak groves throughout the Midwest
    C. sequoia groves of Northern California
    D. pine barrens of New Jersey

24. Each of the following is a factor that affects the erosion of soil by water EXCEPT   24____

    A. volume of precipitation
    B. wind patterns
    C. topography of land
    D. type of vegetational cover

25. Which of the following is classified as an inorganic soil fertilizer?   25____

    A. Legumes   B. Manure   C. Sewage   D. Nitrates

KEY (CORRECT ANSWERS)

1.	B	11.	D
2.	A	12.	A
3.	B	13.	C
4.	C	14.	D
5.	A	15.	B
6.	B	16.	A
7.	A	17.	C
8.	D	18.	A
9.	C	19.	D
10.	C	20.	A

21.	C
22.	B
23.	A
24.	B
25.	D

___

EXAMINATION SECTION
TEST 1

DIRECTIONS: Each question or incomplete statement is followed by several suggested answers or completions. Select the one that BEST answers the question or completes the statement. *PRINT THE LETTER OF THE CORRECT ANSWER IN THE SPACE AT THE RIGHT.*

1. Which of the following materials used in collecting water samples is LEAST likely to contribute contaminants to the sample?   1.____

    A. Glass   B. Teflon
    C. Polypropylene   D. Stainless steel

2. A prepared reference sample, inserted into sample processing as close to the beginning as possible, is known as a(n) _____ sample.   2.____

    A. audit   B. control
    C. continuous   D. blank

3. Which type of sampling plan is based on the judgment of technical experts?   3.____

    A. Intuitive   B. Statistical
    C. Isokinetic   D. Spatial

4. Of the following, the type of *blank* NOT generally used in laboratory analysis is   4.____

    A. solvent   B. system   C. method   D. trip

5. An analyst should MOST strenuously avoid imposing turbulence on water samples that are being tested for   5.____

    A. dissolved solids   B. biotic content
    C. dissolved gases   D. suspended particulates

6. Which of the following is NOT a primary factor in determining the appropriate device to be used in collecting air samples?   6.____

    A. The amount of air to be moved
    B. Altitude of measurement
    C. Opposing vacuum forces
    D. Nature of substance to be analyzed

7. _____ meters is GENERALLY considered to be the shallowest depth in a standing body of water that will assure an analyst of the absence of chemical or thermal stratification.   7.____

    A. 3   B. 5   C. 10   D. 15

8. The FIRST collection of any material for analysis is known as _____ sampling.   8.____

    A. reference   B. primary
    C. dip   D. control

9. The collection technique ESPECIALLY appropriate for sampling rivers for chemical constituents is   9.____

    A. static grab   B. point sampling
    C. spatial gradient   D. stratified dip

10. To insure initial air flow through sampling and analyzing equipment, air pollutant samples should be collected 10.____

    A. on the upstream side of the air mover
    B. as close to the air mover as possible
    C. on the downstream side of the air mover
    D. as far from the air mover as possible

11. The MINIMUM number of samples to be collected from a water distribution system is determined by the 11.____

    A. population served by the system
    B. capacity of the system
    C. linear range of distribution
    D. peak rate of distribution

12. A substance that is being measured or sought in any sample of environmental or chemical matter is called a(n) 12.____

    A. control   B. reagent   C. solvent   D. analyte

13. The volume of air in a high-volume sample is measured in terms of 13.____

    A. cubic meters
    B. proportion of dissolved gases to ambient air
    C. time lapsed during collection
    D. rate of flow through the collection device

14. Which is the BEST season, in temperate regions, to collect samples from lakes in which waters are mixed enough to allow representative readings? 14.____

    A. Winter   B. Spring   C. Summer   D. Fall

15. The standard, generalized method for separating a pollutant for analysis from an air sample is to 15.____

    A. impose gravitational separators
    B. use liquid media
    C. exploit differences in related substances
    D. leave the substances together, but catalog them with separate data

16. The ONLY accurate way to measure the content of waste-water samples is through the analysis of 16.____

    A. specific point samples
    B. grab samples from areas that are well-mixed
    C. samples from both upstream and downstream sides of the dump
    D. composite samples that are proportioned according to flow patterns

17. A pool of two increments that is reduced or prepared as a subsample for analysis is called a 17.____

    A. spike   B. gross sample
    C. control sample   D. continuous sample

18. Of the following, the one which is NOT an advantage associated with the use of static   18.____
    sensors in the collection of air samples is

    A. no requisite human supervision
    B. low cost
    C. high-volume efficiency rate
    D. operation without reliance on electrical power

19. A substance that absorbs and separates a contaminant from the remainder of a sample   19.____
    is a

    A. reactant   B. reagent   C. spike   D. control

20. When wastewater samples are being collected in order to appraise plant performance,   20.____
    the recommended sampling pattern consists of

    A. grab samples from different points during peak flow
    B. grab samples at regular time intervals over a random six-hour period
    C. composite samples over a 24-hour weekday period
    D. daily composite samples over a random seven-day period

21. One DISADVANTAGE associated with the use of dustfall jars for the collection of air sam-   21.____
    ples is

    A. dependence on supervision
    B. limited long-range collection
    C. expensive operation
    D. failure to measure smaller particles

22. The MOST effective method for removing potential contaminants from equipment used in   22.____
    sample collection is

    A. steam washing   B. repeated boiling
    C. inert disinfectants   D. detergent scrubbing

23. The term for a sample value that disagrees in magnitude with its neighboring samples is   23.____

    A. variance   B. spatial outlier
    C. spike   D. range

24. Which of the following is a method for measuring particulate pollution in air samples?   24.____

    A. Bubbling
    B. Adsorption
    C. Introduction of a reactant
    D. Inertial separation

25. Compounds whose presence obscures the measurement of a substance by introducing   25.____
    an unrelated analytical signal are referred to as

    A. interferences   B. controls
    C. toxics   D. blanks

KEY (CORRECT ANSWERS)

1.	B	11.	A
2.	A	12.	D
3.	A	13.	D
4.	D	14.	A
5.	C	15.	C
6.	B	16.	D
7.	B	17.	B
8.	B	18.	C
9.	C	19.	B
10.	A	20.	C

21.	D
22.	A
23.	B
24.	D
25.	A

———

TEST 2

1. To determine the maximum load for a given wastewater treatment unit, an analyst should use _____ samples _____ flow.

    A. grab; collected during peak
    B. integrated; proportioned to the average
    C. integrated; that reflect the range in
    D. integrated; collected during peak

1.____

2. The AVERAGE rate of flow, in cubic feet per minute, through a mechanical air sampler is

    A. 10-20   B. 40-60   C. 100-130   D. 180-200

2.____

3. The obtaining of a representative sample from a flowing stream that contains particulate matter is known as _____ sampling.

    A. stratified   B. intuitive
    C. isokinetic   D. suspended

3.____

4. Of the following situations, the one MOST appropriate for the use of mechanical air samplers is for measuring

    A. a high volume of particulate matter
    B. dissolved gas content
    C. a specific chemical substance
    D. and separating particulate matter by size

4.____

5. The CORRECT term for introduced samples in a procedure that do not contain the substance of interest, but are otherwise composed the same as actual samples, is

    A. controls   B. spikes   C. fields   D. blanks

5.____

6. The number of sampling replications required to sufficient-ly characterize a water body is decided PRIMARILY by the

    A. size of the water body
    B. stratification of the water body
    C. climatic conditions influencing the state of the water body
    D. purpose of the sampling

6.____

7. When sampling is done for the purpose of monitoring quality, sample replication can be expressed in terms of each of the following EXCEPT

    A. confidence limits   B. arithmetic means
    C. expanded controls   D. standard deviations

7.____

8. The MOST common method for measuring the amount of particulate matter in an air sample is   8.____

    A. weighing the sampler's filter before and after collection
    B. recording level of chemical activity with an introduced reactant
    C. determining volume ratios based on the rate of flow
    D. a strictly calibrated volume measurement

9. The use of single point samples in wastewater analysis is considered ACCEPTABLE in the determination of   9.____

    A. the capacity of the system
    B. specific chemical substance content
    C. representative waste flow during operation hours
    D. compliance with discharge regulations

10. Which of the following types of water bodies contains the HIGHEST variability of chemical constituents?   10.____

    A. Freshwater lakes
    B. Near-shore marine environments
    C. Deep, rapidly flowing streams
    D. Shallow, slowly flowing streams

11. The type of sample against which the results of a procedure are judged is known as a(n)   11.____

    A. blank   B. spike   C. control   D. analyte

12. The MOST common method for removing dissolved gases from a given air sample is through   12.____

    A. adsorption with solids
    B. absorption into a liquid medium
    C. inertial separation
    D. filtration

13. In collecting samples from relatively shallow, rapidly flowing streams and rivers, an analyst should be aware that such streams   13.____

    A. contain widely varying constituents at different depths
    B. cannot be representatively sampled
    C. are not consistently stratified
    D. can be sufficiently sampled at one point

14. In sampling wastewater, the term for the time period or volume of waste for which a composite estimate is desired is the   14.____

    A. spatial gradient   B. composite range
    C. minimum range   D. primary sampling unit

15. The type of introduced sample used PRIMARILY by analysts as tools for assessing and controlling sample contamination is   15.____

    A. blanks   B. interferences
    C. reagents   D. controls

16. Which sampling pattern is the MOST commonly used in the monitoring of sewer use?   16.____

    A.   Long-term composite samples at a point far downstream from the discharge
    B.   Grab samples from different critical points in the system
    C.   Composite samples from a point as close to the primary discharge as possible
    D.   Composite samples from different critical points in the system

17. The one of the following sampling/collecting materials MOST likely to contribute a chloro-   17.____
form contaminant to a water sample is

    A.   fiberglas-reinforced epoxy (FRE)
    B.   threaded PVC conduit
    C.   polypropylene
    D.   cemented PVC conduit

18. The MOST common motivation for sealing samples in their collection vessels is   18.____

    A.   analysis of clear biotic potential
    B.   prevention of dissolving particulate matter
    C.   analysis of volatile compound content
    D.   prevention of contamination from ambient air

19. If seasonal variations are of interest in a given water supply, monitoring samples should   19.____
be collected

    A.   hourly   B.   daily   C.   weekly   D.   monthly

20. Which of the following types of *blanks* is NOT generally used in field collecting?   20.____

    A.   Sampling media   B.   Reagent
    C.   Equipment   D.   Matched-matrix

21. The collection medium for MOST high-volume air samplers is a   21.____

    A.   borosilicate glass collection jar
    B.   silica gel absorber
    C.   glass fiber filter
    D.   distilled, inert liquid

22. Of the following situations, the one which is MOST appropriate for the use of static sen-   22.____
sors in the process of collection air samples is for

    A.   collecting a specific volume of air
    B.   separating sample content throughout time gradients
    C.   measuring dissolved gases
    D.   long-term collection of particulates

23. A deep, rapidly flowing river is _____ stratified _____ .   23.____

    A.   usually; into fairly consistent thermal zones
    B.   more likely to be; thermally than chemically
    C.   more likely to be; than a standing body of water
    D.   more likely to be; chemically than thermally

24. The type of sampling plan MOST likely to provide a basis for making probabilistic conclusions that are independent of personal judgment is

    A. statistical   B. isokinetic
    C. primary   D. intuitive

24.____

25. Generally, the BEST location from which to collect representative samples from smooth-flowing rivers that are above any tidal influences is at

    A. the surface   B. near-shore eddies
    C. mid-depth   D. lower depths

25.____

KEY (CORRECT ANSWERS)

1.	D		11.	C
2.	B		12.	B
3.	C		13.	C
4.	A		14.	D
5.	D		15.	A
6.	D		16.	D
7.	C		17.	B
8.	A		18.	C
9.	D		19.	C
10.	B		20.	B

21.	C
22.	D
23.	D
24.	A
25.	C

EXAMINATION SECTION
TEST 1

DIRECTIONS: Each question or incomplete statement is followed by several suggested answers or completions. Select the one that BEST answers the question or completes the statement. *PRINT THE LETTER OF THE CORRECT ANSWER IN THE SPACE AT THE RIGHT.*

1. Which of the following devices is considered to be the MOST effective way of reporting a water supply's chemical composition data?　　1.____

    A. table　　　　　　　　　　　　B. bar graph
    C. cross-referenced spread sheet　　D. circular graph

2. The type of data report which MUST be used as an integral part of any dataprocessing system associated with air quality measurement is　　2.____

    A. data summarization　　　　B. diurnal variation pattern
    C. pollutant rose　　　　　　　D. frequency distribution

3. The term for an analyst's attempt to detect and correct any errors that have entered the data set is data　　3.____

    A. handling　　　　　　B. validation
    C. processing　　　　　D. proofing

4. Of the types of data listed below, which one is NOT used as a parameter to define the physical characteristics of a lake?　　4.____

    A. Surface area　　　　　　　　　B. Average depth
    C. Underlying rock characteristics　D. Retention time

5. The difference between the least and greatest values in a data set is known as the set's　　5.____

    A. variance　　　B. range　　　C. mean deviation　D. mode

6. When experts in the same field disagree about conclusions drawn from a set of environmental impact assessment data, they sometimes privately answer a prepared questionnaire, and then distribute a summary sheet of opposing viewpoints amongst themselves. This method is known as　　6.____

    A. the cooperative assessment model
    B. the Delphi technique
    C. the operational gaming model
    D. collective data validation

7. The term for calculated decrease In water pressure within a delivery system is　　7.____

    A. vacuum　　　B. head loss　　　C. backup　　　D. flow gradient

8. Of the types of environmental impact data variables below, the one which is an example of an output variable is　　8.____

    A. effects on natural and social environments
    B. population projections
    C. transportation networks
    D. economic growth

9. All of the following are factors required for the calculation of flow velocity in water delivery systems EXCEPT   9.____

    A. quantity of flow   B. pipe material
    C. slope of hydraulic gradient   D. temperature of flow

10. _____ errors in a data set are MOST easily estimated by the use of standard statistical techniques.   10.____

    A. Systematic   B. Random   C. Clerical   D. Standard

11. The one of the following which Is NOT an element of the data base needed in order to make decisions about water quality control is the   11.____

    A. physical characteristics of the water resource
    B. local needs and desires concerning use
    C. projected quality of untreated water
    D. present uses of resource

12. The air quality data report that consists of collected averages for a specific daily time period is the   12.____

    A. pollutant rose   B. data summarization
    C. diurnal variation pattern   D. frequency distribution

13. The concentration of bacteriological wastes in water is USUALLY expressed in terms of   13.____

    A. parts per million
    B. specific particle ratios, depending on the waste
    C. kiloPascals
    D. BOD

14. The one of the characteristics below that Is NOT used as a criterion for determining the quality of a data set is   14.____

    A. flexibility   B. representativeness
    C. comparability   D. completeness

15. In water delivery systems, water pressure is USUALLY measured in units called   15.____

    A. meters of head   B. pounds per square inch
    C. flow gradients   D. Pascals

16. In measuring air quality, extremes in data are often due to each of the following EXCEPT   16.____

    A. meteorological factors   B. clerical misrecordings
    C. lab errors   D. saturation of continuous data

17. The term for the difference between a data set's MEASURED and REFERENCED values is   17.____

    A. accuracy   B. quantitative error
    C. reliability   D. precision

18. In order to determine the storage needed to equalize a community's water supply demand at a constant pumping pressure, the MOST important data set needed is the   18.____

    A. exact pumping pressure
    B. time of daily peak use
    C. community's consumption rate
    D. delivery time between source and key use stations

19. _____ is the MOST commonly used method for determining the central value of a given data set.   19.____

    A. Mid-range   B. Mode
    C. Arithmetic mean   D. Median

20. What is the method for determining the standard deviation of values in a data set?   20.____

    A. Square root of the variance
    B. Half the total variance
    C. Average of all deviating values
    D. Average of the square roots of all deviating values

21. The MOST commonly used device for recording and reporting water delivery data at household sites is the   21.____

    A. compound meter   B. digital register
    C. current meter   D. disk meter

22. The term for the air quality data report that summarizes how often concentrations of specific magnitudes occur is   22.____

    A. frequency distribution   B. data summarization
    C. pollutant rose   D. diurnal variation pattern

23. Regarding environmental impact assessment, the goal of relating input and output variables in a data set is to   23.____

    A. validate the data set
    B. understand the consequences of imposing alternative policies
    C. establish a consensus about policy objectives
    D. compile an adequately useful data set

24. In order to calculate the intake capacity for a fire flow water delivery system, an analyst should compare the system's   24.____

    A. average pressure to the average distance of delivery
    B. total storage to the maximum amount of water needed
    C. maximum pressure to the maximum distance of delivery
    D. total storage to the average amount of water needed

25. Which of the distorting factors below is almost EXCLUSIVELY involved with the presentation of data, rather than the documentation?   25.____

    A. Mechanical error   B. Bias
    C. Meteorological factors   D. Clerical error

KEY (CORRECT ANSWERS)

1.	B	11.	C	
2.	A	12.	C	
3.	B	13.	D	
4.	C	14.	A	
5.	B	15.	A	
6.	B	16.	D	
7.	B	17.	A	
8.	A	18.	C	
9.	D	19.	C	
10.	B	20.	A	

21. D
22. A
23. B
24. B
25. B

———

TEST 2

DIRECTIONS: Each, question or incomplete statement is followed by several suggested answers or completions. Select the one that BEST answers the question or completes the statement. *PRINT THE LETTER OF THE CORRECT ANSWER IN THE SPACE AT THE RIGHT.*

1. The determination of a drinking water supply's conformity with established bacteriological requirements is based on   1.____

   A. comparisons with dissolved solids data
   B. correlated oxygen content
   C. average measurement readings of all tests performed
   D. the number of positive tests

2. The magnitude of error associated with a particular data set is known as   2.____

   A. systematic error   B. data quality
   C. standard variance   D. standard error

3. Which type of air quality data report uses a circular figure for presentation, rather than a table or graph?   3.____

   A. Diurnal variation pattern
   B. Pollutant rose
   C. Frequency distribution
   D. Data summarization

4. When the water pressure within a delivery system is greater than the atmospheric pressure, it is called   4.____

   A. gage pressure   B. barometric pressure
   C. vacuum   D. absolute pressure

5. In data evaluation, the term for the variability of measurements of the same quantity gathered using the same method is   5.____

   A. standard deviation   B. precision
   C. accuracy   D. data variability

6. The data used as the PRIMARY criterion for determining the amount of an allowable Industrial waste dump into a flowing stream is   6.____

   A. external climatic factors
   B. projected flow of the watercourse
   C. biotic potential of surrounding waters
   D. toxicity of waste material

7. Once the data have been gathered for an environmental impact assessment, experts play a prominent role in each of the following ways, EXCEPT   7.____

   A. identifying alternatives and control variables
   B. relating input to output variables
   C. gathering more data using techniques of greater refinement
   D. evaluating reliability and applicability of data

8. In determining the quality of a given water sample, concentrations of dissolved elements are expressed in terms of: 8.____

    A. volume   B. mass
    C. particle ratios   D. surface area

9. The errors in a data set that CANNOT be estimated by the use of standard statistical techniques, and usually produce a biased result, are called _____ errors.   9.____

    A. systematic   B. random
    C. clerical   D. standard

10. The method for data presentation MOST commonly used to illustrate the relationship between two sets of continuous data is the   10.____

    A. bar chart   B. histogram
    C. block graph   D. scatter diagram

11. _____ consumption is NOT part of the data set needed to quantitatively evaluate a community's water use.   11.____

    A. Average daily   B. Peak hourly
    C. Peak daily   D. Average hourly

12. The precision of a data set is BEST expressed in terms of   12.____

    A. mode   B. standard deviation
    C. average   D. frequency

13. In water delivery systems, the use of a manometer for measuring water pressure is   13.____

    A. usually limited to indoor, fixed units
    B. a universally adopted practice
    C. most commonly applied to mobile units
    D. seldom used indoors

14. All of the following are problems often associated with the practice of intermittently collecting air quality data EXCEPT   14.____

    A. inaccurate averages
    B. increased likelihood of extreme values
    C. greater meteorological impact on data
    D. increased susceptibility to error

15. Which of the following Is NOT a method used to measure variation within a data set?   15.____

    A. Mean deviation   B. Standard deviation
    C. Range   D. Variance mode

16. The device MOST commonly used to report pipe flow data for a water delivery system is the   16.____

    A. table   B. circular graph
    C. cross-referenced spread sheet   D. nomograph

17. Of the following, the one which is NOT a problem often associated with using the opera-   17.____
    tional gaming model for evaluating environmental impact assessment data is

    A. distancing of interested parties
    B. increased adventurousness of field experts
    C. introduction of human behavioral patterns into the assessment
    D. possibly inaccurate idealization of the system

18. The chemical analysis of a water sample can be used to determine each of the following   18.____
    factors EXCEPT

    A. dissolved solids   B. alkalinity
    C. biotic potential   D. pH

19. The air quality data report that groups data according to prevailing wind directions is the   19.____

    A. frequency distribution   B. pollutant rose
    C. diurnal variation pattern   D. data summarization

20. The MOST commonly used device for measuring water pressure in delivery systems is   20.____
    the

    A. piezometer   B. Bourdon gauge
    C. manometer   D. barometric gauge

21. Each of the following is a problem associated with the use of existing data In making   21.____
    environmental impact assessments EXCEPT the

    A. possibility of different gathering techniques
    B. uncertainty of data accuracy due to time lapse
    C. unsuitabillty of data for an analyst's specific purpose
    D. personal bias of the analyst using the data

22. The data presentation method that works BEST for illustrating frequency distributions is   22.____
    the

    A. compass graph   B. table
    C. histogram   D. bar graph

23. The _____ is NOT a factor required in order to calculate storm runoff.   23.____

    A. maximum flow rate
    B. area's average rainfall intensity
    C. type and character of runoff surface
    D. minimum flow rate

24. Which of the characteristics of a data set is almost EXCLUSIVELY involved in the docu-   24.____
    mentation of values, rather than the presentation?

    A. Accuracy   B. Representativeness
    C. Bias   D. Comparability

25. The MOST frequently appearing valuc in a data set is known as its   25.____

    A. variance standard   B. mode
    C. mid-range   D. median

KEY (CORRECT ANSWERS)

1.	D	11.	D
2.	B	12.	B
3.	B	13.	A
4.	A	14.	C
5.	B	15.	D
6.	B	16.	D
7.	C	17.	A
8.	B	18.	C
9.	A	19.	B
10.	D	20.	B

21. D
22. C
23. D
24. A
25. B

EXAMINATION SECTION
TEST 1

DIRECTIONS: Each question or incomplete statement is followed by several suggested answers or completions. Select the one that *BEST* answers the question or completes the statement. *PRINT THE LETTER OF THE CORRECT ANSWER IN THE SPACE AT THE RIGHT.*

1. When 60,987 is added to 27,835, the result is

    A. 80,712   B. 80,822   C. 87,712   D. 88,822

1.____

2. The sum of 693 + 787 + 946 + 355 + 731 is

    A. 3,512   B. 3,502   C. 3,412   D. 3,402

2.____

3. When 2,586 is subtracted from 3,003, the result is

    A. 417   B. 527   C. 1,417   D. 1,527

3.____

4. When 1.32 is subtracted from 52.6, the result is

    A. 3.94   B. 5.128   C. 39.4   D. 51.28

4.____

5. When 56 is multiplied by 438, the result is

    A. 840   B. 4,818   C. 24,528   D. 48,180

5.____

6. When 8.7 is multiplied by .34, the result is, most nearly,

    A. 2.9   B. 3.0   C. 29.5   D. 29.6

6.____

7. When 1/2 is divided by 2/3, the result is

    A. 1/3   B. 3/4   C. 1 1/3   D. 3

7.____

8. When 8,340 is divided by 38, the result is, most nearly

    A. 210   B. 218   C. 219   D. 220

8.____

Questions 9-11.

DIRECTIONS: Questions 9 to 11 inclusive are to be answered *SOLELY* on the basis of the information given below.

Assume that a certain water treatment plant has consumed quantities of chemicals E and F over a five-week period, as indicated in the following table:

Time Period	Number of 100-pound sacks consumed	
	Chemical E	Chemical F
Week 1	5	4
Week 2	7	5
Week 3	6	5
Week 4	8	6
Week 5	6	4

9. The *total* number of pounds of chemical E consumed at the end of the first three weeks is   9.____

    A.   180   B.   320   C.   1,400   D.   1,800

10. According to the table, the week in which the *most* chemicals were consumed was   10.____

    A. week 2   B. week 3   C. week 4   D. week 5

11. According to the table, the *average* number of sacks of chemical F consumed over the   11.____
first four weeks was

    A. 4   B. 5   C. 6   D. 7

12. Of the following actions, the *best* one to take *FIRST* after smoke is seen coming from an   12.____
electric control device is to

    A.   shut off the power to it
    B.   call the main office for advice
    C.   look for a wiring diagram
    D.   throw water on it

13. Of the following items, the one which would *LEAST* likely be included on a memorandum   13.____
is the

    A.   home address of the writer of the memorandum
    B.   name of the writer of the memorandum
    C.   subject of the memorandum
    D.   names or titles of the person who will receive the memorandum

14. When testing joints for leaks in pipe lines containing natural gas, it is *BEST* to use   14.____

    A.   water in the lines under pressure
    B.   a lighted candle
    C.   an aquastat
    D.   soapy water

Questions 15-17.

DIRECTIONS: Questions 15 to 17 inclusive are to be answered *SOLELY* on the basis of the
information given below.

    Assume that at various hours of a typical day the amounts of chlorine residual in parts
per million (ppm) at a certain water treatment plant are as shown in the following graph:

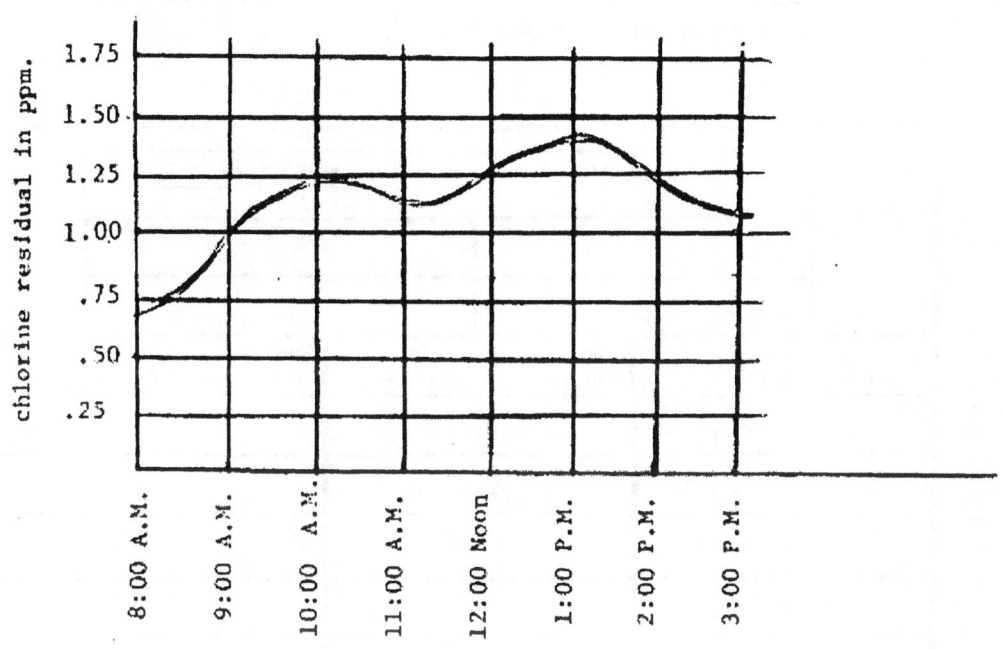

15. According to the graph, the chlorine residual measured in ppm at 9:00 A.M. was, most nearly,   15.____

    A. .70   B. .75   C. 1.00   D. 1.25

16. The maximum chlorine residual between 8:00 A.M. and 3:00 P.M. was, most nearly,   16.____

    A. .68 ppm   B. 1.10 ppm   C. 1.25 ppm   D. 1.37 ppm

17. According to the graph, between the hour of 12:00 Noon and 1:00 P.M., the chlorine residual was   17.____

    A. always increasing   B. always decreasing
    C. increasing, then decreasing   D. decreasing, then increasing

18. Of the following statements concerning the use and care of wooden ladders, the *one* which is *TRUE* is that   18.____

    A. a light oil should be applied to the rungs to preserve the wood
    B. each rung should be sharply struck with a metal hammer to test its soundness before using it
    C. ladders should be stored in a warm damp area to prevent the wood from getting brittle
    D. tops of ordinary stepladders should not be used as steps

19. It is *poor* practice to use gasoline to clean metal parts that are coated with grease *PRIMARILY* because gasoline   19.____

    A. contains lead which is harmful to the user
    B. is a poor solvent for grease
    C. corrodes metal
    D. vapors ignite easily

Questions 20-21.

DIRECTIONS   Questions 20 and 21 are to be answered *SOLELY* on the basis of the information given in the tables below.

Inventory of 100 pound bags on hand as of 1-1	
Chemical X	16 1/2
Chemical Y	12

Date	Chemical	Number of 100 pound bags used	Number of 100 pound bags received
1-5	X	8 1/2	
1-9	X	3 1/2	
1-9	Y	5	
1-14	X		8
1-18	Y	2 1/2	
1-23	X	3	
1-27	Y	4 1/2	
1-30	X		2
1-31	X	1	

Inventory of 100 pound bags on hand as of 1-31	
Chemical X	
Chemical Y	

J. Doe	2-2
Operator	

20. According to the information given in the table, the number of 100-pound bags of chemical Y *on hand* as of 1-31 is   20._____

   A. 0   B. 1/2   C. 1   D. 1 1/2

21. According to the information in the table, the *total* number of pounds of chemical X consumed in the month was, most nearly,   21._____

   A. 500   B. 1,600   C. 1,800   D. 2,800

Questions 22-27.

DIRECTIONS: Questions 22 to 27 inclusive are to be answered *SOLELY* on the basis of the paragraph below.

FIRST AID INSTRUCTIONS

The main purpose of first aid is to put the injured person in the best possible position until medical help arrives. This includes the performance of emergency treatment for the purpose of saving a life if a doctor is not present. When a person is hurt, a crowd usually gathers around the victim. If nobody uses his head, the injured person fails to get the care he needs. You must stay calm and, most important, it is your duty to take charge at an accident. The first thing for you to do is to see, as best you can, what is wrong with the injured person. Leave the victim where he is until the nature and extent of his injury are determined. If he is unconscious he should not be moved except to lay him flat on his back if he is in some other position. Loosen the clothing of any seriously hurt person and make him as comfortable as possible. Medical help should be called as soon as possible. You should remain with the injured person and send someone else to call the doctor. You should try to make sure that the one who calls for a doctor is able to give correct information as to the location of the injured person. In order to help the physician to know what equipment may be needed in each particular case, the person making the call should give the doctor as much information about the injury as possible.

22. If nobody uses his head at the scene of an accident, there is danger that   22.____

    A. no one will get the names of all the witnesses
    B. a large crowd will gather
    C. the victim will not get the care he needs
    D. the victim will blame the City for negligence

23. When an accident occurs, the *FIRST* thing you should do is   23.____

    A. call a doctor
    B. loosen the clothing of the injured person
    C. notify the victim's family
    D. try to find out what is wrong with the injured person

24. If you do *NOT* know the extent and nature of the victim's injuries, you should   24.____

    A. let the injured person lie where he is
    B. immediately take the victim to a hospital yourself
    C. help the injured person to his feet to see if he can walk
    D. have the injured person sit up on the ground while you examine him

25. If the injured person is breathing and unconscious, you should   25.____

    A. get some hot liquid such as coffee or tea in to him
    B. give him artificial respiration
    C. lift up his head to try to stimulate blood circulation
    D. see that he lies flat on his back

26. If it is necessary to call a doctor, you should   26._____

    A. go and make the call yourself since you have all the information
    B. find out who the victim's family doctor is before making the call
    C. have someone else make the call who knows the location of the victim
    D. find out which doctor the victim can afford

27. It is important for the caller to give the doctor as much information as is available regard-   27._____
     ing the injury so that the doctor

    A. can bring the necessary equipment
    B. can make out an accident report
    C. will be responsible for any malpractice resulting from the first aid treatment
    D. can inform his nurse on how long he will be in the field

Questions 28-29.

DIRECTIONS: Questions 28 and 29 are to be answered SOLELY on the basis of the para-
               graph below.

When a written report must be submitted by an operator to his supervisor, the best rule is
"the briefer the better." Obviously, this can be carried to extremes, since all necessary information must be included. However, the ability to write a satisfactory one-page report is an
important communication skill. There are several different kinds of reports in common use.
One is the form report, which is printed and merely requires the operator to fill in blanks. The
greatest problems faced in completion of this report are accuracy and thoroughness. Another
type of report is one that must be submitted regularly and systematically. This type of report is
known as the periodic report.

28. According to the passage above, accuracy and thoroughness are the GREATEST prob-   28 _____
     lems in the completion of

    A. one-page reports   B. form reports
    C. periodic reports   D. long reports

29. According to the passage above, a good written report from an operator to his supervisor   29._____
     should be

    A. printed
    B. formal
    C. periodic
    D. brief

Question 30.

DIRECTIONS: The sketches below show 150-lb. chlorine cylinders stored in three different
               ways:

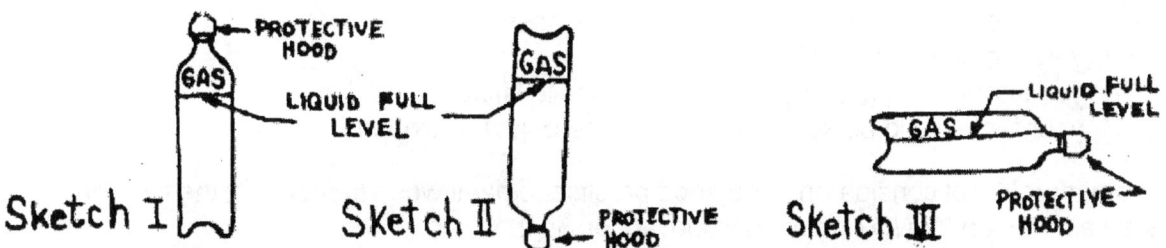

30. *Recommended* practice is to store a 150-lb. chlorine cylinder as shown in   30.____

    A. Sketch I *only*   B. Sketch II *only*
    C. Sketch III *only*   D. Sketches II and III

31. Of the following, the *MOST* serious defect in the installation shown below is that   31.____

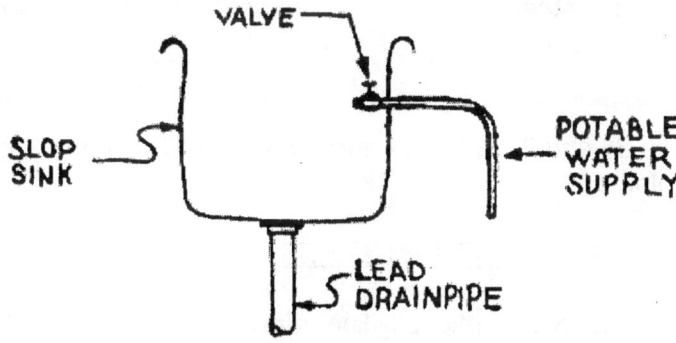

    A. the water supply should be directed downward to prevent excessive splashing over the rim
    B. the above installation may allow backflow of waste water into the water supply line
    C. lead pipes should not be used on drains from fixtures connected to the potable water supply
    D. excessive corrosion will occur on the valve if it becomes submerged

32. Of the following, the distance "x" which would be *SAFEST* when using the extension ladder shown in the sketch below is   32.____

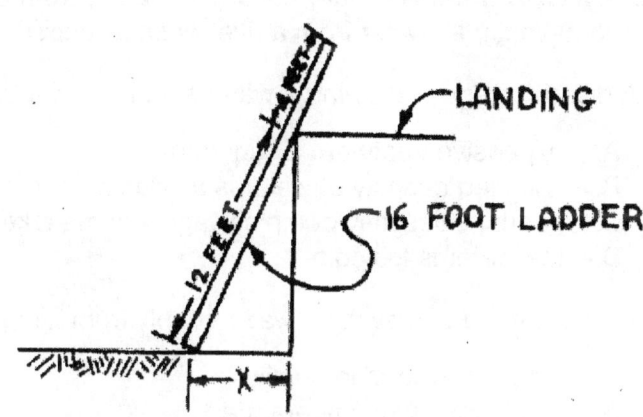

    A. 1 foot   B. 3 feet   C. 5 feet   D. 7 fee

33. Of the following statements regarding safe procedures for lifting a heavy object by yourself from the floor, the one which is *FALSE* is that

    A. you should keep your back as straight as possible
    B. you should bend your knees
    C. you should mainly use your back muscles in lifting
    D. your feet should be kept clear in case the object is dropped

33._____

34. It is generally not considered to be good practice to paint wood ladders. Of the following,
the *best* reason for *NOT* painting wood ladders is that

    A. it may hide defects in the wood
    B. the rungs become slippery
    C. the hardware on the ladder becomes unworkable
    D. it would rub off on the surfaces against which it is resting

34._____

35. A rip saw would *MOST* likely be used to cut

    A. wood   B. steel   C. copper   D. aluminum

35._____

Questions 36-37.

DIRECTIONS: Questions 36 and 37 are to be answered *SOLELY* on the basis of the paragraph below.

NATURAL LAKES

Large lakes may yield water of exceptionally fine quality except near the shore line and in
the vicinity of sewer outlets or near outlets of large streams. Therefore, minimum treatment is
required. The availability of practically unlimited quantities of water is also a decided advantage. Unfortunately, however, the sewage from a city is often discharged into the same lake
from which the water supply is taken. Great care must be taken in locating both the water
intake and the sewer outlet so that the pollution handled by the water treatment plant is a minimum.

Sometimes the distance from the shore where dependable, satisfactory water can be
found is so great that the cost of water intake facilities is prohibitive for a small municipality. In
such cases, another supply must be found, or water must be obtained from a neighboring
large city. Lake water is usually uniform in quality from day to day and does not vary in temperature as much as water from a river or small impounding reservoir.

36. A disadvantage of drawing a water supply from a large lake is that

    A. expensive treatment is required
    B. a limited quantity of water is available
    C. nearby cities may dump sewage into the lake
    D. the water is too cold.

36._____

37. An advantage of drawing a water supply from a large lake is that the

    A. water is uniform in quality
    B. water varies in temperature
    C. intake is distant from the shore
    D. intake may be near a sewer outlet

37._____

38. The *BEST* type of wrench to use to tighten a pipe without marring the pipe surface is   38._____

    A. pipe wrench   B. strap wrench
    C. spanner wrench   D. box wrench

39. Of the following statements concerning the use and care of files, the *one* which is *FALSE*   39._____
is that

    A. files should have tight-fitting handles
    B. rasps are generally used on wood
    C. files should be protected by a light coating of oil when cutting metal
    D. files should be given a quick blow on a wood block to unclog teeth

40. A device which permits flow of a fluid in a pipe in one direction only is known as   40._____

    A. diode   B. curb box
    C. gooseneck   D. check valve

KEY (CORRECT ANSWERS)

1.	D	11.	B	21.	B	31.	B
2.	A	12.	A	22.	C	32.	B
3.	A	13.	A	23.	D	33.	C
4.	D	14.	D	24.	A	34.	A
5.	C	15.	C	25.	D	35.	A
6.	B	16.	D	26.	C	36.	C
7.	B	17.	A	27.	A	37.	A
8.	C	18.	D	28.	B	38.	B
9.	D	19.	D	29.	D	39.	C
10.	C	20.	A	30.	A	40.	D

TEST 2

DIRECTIONS: Each question or incomplete statement is followed by several suggested answers or completions. Select the one that *BEST* answers the question or completes the statement. *PRINT THE LETTER OF THE CORRECT ANSWER IN THE SPACE AT THE RIGHT.*

Questions 1-2.

DIRECTIONS: Questions 1 and 2 are to be answered *SOLELY* on the basis of the paragraph below.

PRECIPITATION AND RUNOFF

In the United States, the average annual precipitation is about 30 inches, of which about 21 inches is lost to the atmosphere by evaporation and transpiration. The remaining 9 inches becomes runoff into rivers and lakes. Both the precipitation and runoff vary greatly with geography and season. Annual precipitation varies from more than 100 inches in parts of the northwest to only 2 or 3 inches in parts of the southwest. In the northeastern part of the country, including New York State, the annual average precipitation is about 45 inches, of which about 22 inches becomes runoff. Even in New York State, there is some variation from place to place and considerable variation from time to time. During extremely dry years, the precipitation may be as low as 30 inches and the runoff below 10 inches. In general, there are greater variations in runoff rates from smaller watersheds. A critical water supply situation occurs when there are three or four abnormally dry years in succession.

Precipitation over the state is measured and recorded by a net-work of stations operated by the U. S. Weather Bureau. All of the precipitation records and other data such as temperature, humidity and evaporation rates are published monthly by the Weather Bureau in "Climatological Data." Runoff rates at more than 200 stream-gauging stations in the state are measured and recorded by the U. S. Geological Survey in cooperation with various state agencies. Records of the daily average flows are published annually by the U. S. Geological Survey in "Surface Water Records of New York." Copies may be obtained by writing to the Water Resources Division, United States Geological Survey, Albany, New York 23301.

1. From the above paragraphs it is *appropriate* to conclude that   1.____

    A. critical supply situations do not occur
    B. the greater the rainfall, the greater the runoff
    C. there are greater variations in runoff from larger watersheds
    D. the rainfall in the southwest is greater than the average in the country

2. From the above paragraphs, it is appropriate to conclude that   2.____

    A. an annual rainfall of about 50 inches does not occur in New York State
    B. the U. S. Weather Bureau is only interested in rainfall
    C. runoff is equal to rainfall less losses to the atmosphere
    D. information about rainfall and runoff in New York State is unavailable to the public

3. The following are diagrams of various types of bolt heads.

The *one* of the above which is a Phillips head type is the one labelled
A. A   B. B   C. C   D. D

4. The appearance of frost on the outer surface of a chlorine cylinder which has been placed in service would *MOST* likely indicate that

   A. the cylinder is empty
   B. the gas is escaping too quickly from the cylinder
   C. there is too much pressure in the cylinder
   D. the humidity of the storage area is too high

5. One of the outer belts of a matched set of three V-belts becomes badly frayed. Of the following, the *BEST* course of action to take is to

   A. replace only the worn belt
   B. replace only the worn belt but put the new belt in the middle
   C. remove the worn belt, put the center belt on the end and continue running the machine
   D. replace the whole set of belts even if the other two belts show no signs of wear\

6. Of the following, the *BEST* type of valve to use for throttling or when the valve must be opened and closed frequently is a

   A. check valve   B. globe valve
   C. butterfly valve   D. pop valve

7. Of the following, the device which is used to measure *both* pressure and vacuum is the

   A. compound gage   B. aquastat
   C. pyrometer   D. thermocouple

8. Electrical energy is consumed and paid for in units of

   A. voltage   B. ampere-hours
   C. kilowatt-hours   D. watts

9. A "governor" on an engine is used to control the engine's

   A. speed   B. temperature
   C. interval of operation
   D. engaging and disengaging the "load"

10. Pressure *below* that of the atmospheric pressure is usually expressed in

   A. vacuum inches of mercury   B. inches of pressure absolute
   C. BTU's   D. gallons per minute

11.   A short piece of pipe with outside threads at both ends is called a   11._____

      A. union   B. nipple   C. tee   D. sleeve

12.   Of the following, which device would *MOST* likely produce water hammer in a plumbing   12._____
      installation? A(n)

      A. relief valve   B. air chamber
      C. surge tank   D. quick-closing valve

13.   Some portable electric tools have a third conductor in the line cord which is electrically   13._____
      connected to the receptacle box. The reason for this is to

      A. have a spare wire in case one power wire breaks
      B. protect the user of the tool from electrical shock
      C. strengthen the power lead so that it cannot be easily damaged
      D. allow use of the tool for extended periods of time without overheating

14.   Of the following, the device which is usually used to measure the rate of flow of water in a   14._____
      pipe is a

      A. pressure gage   B. Bourden gage
      C. manometer   D. velocity meter

15.   Acid, rosin fluid, or paste applied to metal surfaces to remove oxide film in preparation for   15._____
      soldering is known as

      A. grout   B. lampblack   C. plumber's soil   D. flux

16.   In plumbing work, a coil spring which is inserted into a drain to facilitate cleaning of the   16._____
      drain is known as a

      A. pipe reamer   B. snake   C. plunger   D. spigot

17.   Of the following, a pneumatic device is one that is driven or powered by   17._____

      A. air pressure   B. oil pressure
      C. water pressure   D. steam pressure

18.   Of the following metals, the one which would *MOST* likely be used for an electric motor   18._____
      shaft is

      A. wrought iron   B. hard bronze
      C. steel   D. bras

19.   Of the following, a rotary gear pump is *BEST* suited for pumping   19._____

      A. #6 fuel oil   B. hot water   C. sewage   D. kerosene

20.   The *MAIN* reason for using a flexible coupling to join the shafts of two pieces of machin-   20._____
      ery together is that a flexible coupling

      A. allows for slight misalignment of the two shafts
      B. can be immediately disengaged in an emergency
      C. will automatically slip when overloaded thus protecting the driver machinery
      D. allows the driven load shaft to continue rotating under its own momentum, when
          the driver shaft is stopped

21. Of the following, the MAIN purpose of a house trap is to

    A. provide the house drain with a cleanout
    B. prevent gases from the public sewer from entering the house plumbing system
    C. trap articles of value that are accidentally dropped into the drainage pipes
    D. eliminate the necessity for traps under all other plumbing fixtures

21.____

22. Of the following, the MAIN reason for sometimes applying bituminous coating to the interiors of steel and cast-iron pipe is that this coating

    A. increases the tensile strength of the pipe
    B. increases the shock resistance of the pipe
    C. removes any objectionable taste from the water imparted by the pipe walls
    D. protects the pipe walls from corrosion

22.____

23. The one of the following electrical devices which is most likely to be used to raise or lower A.C. voltages is a

    A. resistor   B. thermistor   C. transformer   D. circuit-breaker

23.____

24. When a metal is galvanized, it is given a coating of

    A. nickel   B. tin   C. oxide   D. zinc

24.____

25. A conduit hickey is used to

    A. measure conduit pipe   B. bend conduit pipe
    C. thread conduit pipe   D. cut conduit pipe

25.____

Questions 26-27.

DIRECTIONS: Questions 26 and 27 are to be answered SOLELY on the basis of the electrical circuit shown below.

26. The circuit above is commonly known as a

    A. series circuit   B. parallel circuit
    C. short circuit   D. circuit breaker

26.____

27. The current flowing in the circuit above is

    A. 1 amp   B. 2 amps   C. 3 amps   D. 6 amps

27.____

Questions 28-30.

DIRECTIONS: Questions 28 to 30 inclusive are to be answered *SOLELY* on the basis of the sketches shown below.

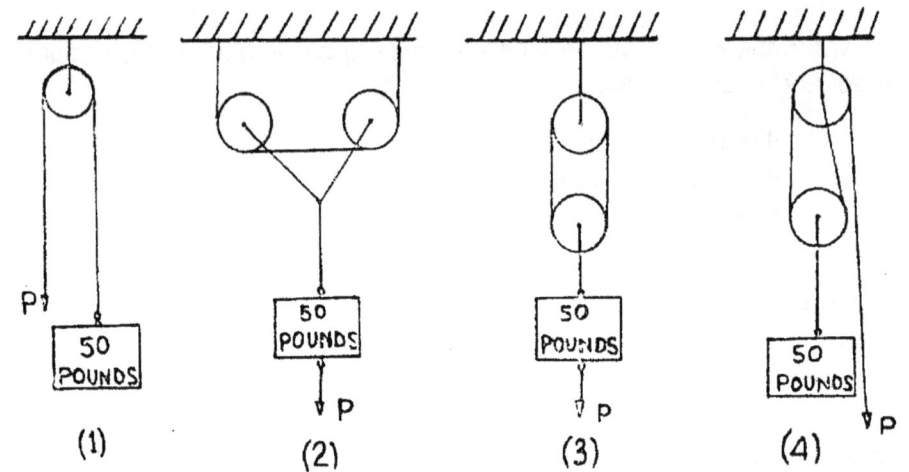

(1)   (2)   (3)   (4)

28.   The two arrangements in the above diagrams which *CANNOT* be used to raise the load   28.____
      at all by applying a pull "p" as shown are setups

      A.   1 and 2   B.   2 and 3   C.   3 and 4   D.   1 and 4

29.   The arrangement in the diagram above which requires the *LEAST* effort "p" to move the   29.____
      50-pound weight is setup

      A.   1   B.   2   C.   3   D.   4

30.   The effort required to hold the 50-pound weight at rest off the ground in setup (1) in the   30.____
      diagram above is

      A.   10 pounds   B.   25 pounds   C.   50 pounds   D.   100 pounds

31.   Of the following formulas, the one which *CORRECTLY* shows the relationship between   31.____
      gage pressure and absolute pressure is

      A.   Absolute pressure = gage pressure / atmospheric pressure
      B.   Absolute pressure + gage pressure = atmospheric pressure
      C.   Absolute pressure = gage pressure + atmospheric pressure
      D.   Absolute pressure + atmospheric pressure = gage pressure

32.   The weight of a gallon of water is, most nearly,   32.____

      A.   8.3 pounds   B.   16.6 pounds   C.   24.9 pounds   D.   33.2 pounds

33.   Solenoid valves are usually operated   33.____

      A.   thermally   B.   manually   C.   hydraulically   D.   electrically

34.   A 1/2-inch, 8-32 round-head machine screw has   34.____

      A.   a diameter of 1/2 inch   B.   a length of 8 inches
      C.   8 threads per inch   D.   32 threads per inch

35. The *MAIN* purpose for the stuffing usually found in centrifugal pump stuffing boxes is   35.____

    A. supporting the shaft
    B. controlling the rate of discharge
    C. preventing fluid leakage
    D. compensating for shaft misalignment

36. The *BEST* wrench to use on screwed valves and fittings having hexagonal shape con-   36.____
nections is the

    A. chain wrench   B. open-end wrench
    C. pipe wrench   D. strap wrench

37. A tap is a tool commonly used to   37.____

    A. remove broken screws   B. flare pipe ends
    C. cut external threads   D. cut internal threads

38. A thread chaser is *MOST* likely to be used to   38.____

    A. rethread damaged threads   B. remove broken taps
    C. flare tubing   D. adjust diestocks

39. If an air-conditioning unit shorted out and caught fire, the *BEST* fire extinguisher to use   39.____
would be a

    A. water extinguisher
    B. foam extinguisher
    C. carbon dioxide extinguisher
    D. soda acid extinguisher

40. Of the following, the *best* action to take to help someone whose eyes have been   40.____
splashed with lye is to *FIRST*

    A. wash out the eyes with clean water
    B. wash out the eyes with a salt water solution
    C. apply a sterile dressing over the eyes
    D. do nothing to the eyes, but telephone for medical help

----

KEY (CORRECT ANSWERS)

1.	B	11.	B	21.	B	31.	C
2.	C	12.	D	22.	D	32.	A
3.	C	13.	B	23.	C	33.	D
4.	B	14.	D	24.	D	34.	D
5.	D	15.	D	25.	B	35.	C
6.	B	16.	B	26.	A	36.	B
7.	A	17.	A	27.	B	37.	D
8.	C	18.	C	28.	B	38.	A
9.	A	19.	A	29.	D	39.	C
10.	A	20.	A	30.	C	40.	A

EXAMINATION SECTION
TEST 1

DIRECTIONS: Each question or incomplete statement is followed by several suggested answers or completions. Select the one that BEST answers the question or completes the statement. *PRINT THE LETTER OF THE CORRECT ANSWER IN THE SPACE AT THE RIGHT.*

1. Rain is MOST directly associated with which one of the following cloud types?   1.____

    A. Cirrus   B. Cumulus   C. Stratus   D. Nimbus

2. Two samples of air MUST have the same dew point if they have the same   2.____

    A. relative humidity   B. absolute humidity
    C. lapse rate   D. capacity

3. In the continental United States of America, wind pressure systems USUALLY move   3.____

    A. westward and more rapidly in winter than in summer
    B. eastward and more rapidly in winter than in summer
    C. eastward at the same number of miles per day in winter as in summer
    D. northeast at 400 miles per day

4. Winds in low pressure systems in continental United States of America blow in which one   4.____
of the following directions?

    A. Clockwise and outward
    B. Counterclockwise toward the center
    C. Counterclockwise and outward
    D. Clockwise and toward the center

5. Assuming proper temperatures, which one of the following crops grows BEST in clay   5.____
soil?

    A. Wheat   B. Peanuts   C. Tobacco   D. Cotton

6. The name given to a violent circular windstorm of small area is which one of the follow-   6.____
ing?

    A. Chinook   B. Tornado   C. Cyclone   D. Anticyclone

7. Which one of the following expressions includes the three others?   7.____

    A. Monsoons   B. Southeast trades
    C. Terrestrial winds   D. Prevailing northwesterlies

8. Highest tides occur soon after the time of which one of the following?   8.____

    A. New moon   B. First quarter moon
    C. Last quarter moon   D. None of the above

9. If the tide is lowest at 3 P.M., it will be HIGHEST thereafter at approximately   9.____

    A. 3 A.M.   B. 6 P.M.   C. 9 P.M.   D. 12 P.M.

10. The GREATEST ocean depths are found in the _____ Ocean.   10._____

    A. Atlantic   B. Pacific   C. Indian   D. Antarctic

11. Which one of the following elements is commercially extracted in large quantity from   11._____
ocean water?

    A. Radium   B. Gold   C. Magnesium   D. Zinc

12. Large-scale ocean currents are caused by   12._____

    A. erosion   B. winds
    C. boat traffic   D. tidal waves

13. Coney Island is an example of which one of the following? A(n)   13._____

    A. barrier beach   B. atoll
    C. levee   D. spit

14. The leeward side of mountains on an island is   14._____

    A. windy   B. dry   C. moist   D. cold

15. The actual mass of water vapor per cubic foot of air is called   15._____

    A. relative humidity   B. absolute humidity
    C. dew point   D. water equivalent

16. Relative humidity is measured by which one of the following?   16._____

    A. An anemometer
    B. Dew point apparatus
    C. Wet and dry bulb thermometer
    D. Maximum and minimum thermometer

17. At 68° F, the relative humidity BEST for human comfort is about   17._____

    A. 20%   B. 35%   C. 50%   D. 80%

18. The horse latitudes are CORRECTLY defined as   18._____

    A. regions of abundant rainfall
    B. belts of high pressure between the trade wind belts and the westerlies
    C. belts of light winds, calms, and high temperature at the equator
    D. wind belts between the westerlies and polar easterlies

19. The irregular line on the map in the doldrum belt passing through places with the HIGH-   19._____
EST temperatures is called

    A. an isotherm   B. the heat equator
    C. a temperature gradient   D. an insolation line

20. Of the following, the type of cloud associated with very high altitude is   20._____

    A. altostratus   B. cirrus
    C. altocumulus   D. cumulonimbus

21. Up to an elevation of 3 to 4 miles at the poles and 10 to 11 miles at the equator, the lapse rate indicates that the temperature of stationary air   21.____

   A. *decreases* at the average rate of 3 1/2 degrees Fahrenheit for each 1000 ft. elevation
   B. *decreases* 3 degrees Fahrenheit for each 100 feet of elevation
   C. *decreases* 10 degrees Fahrenheit for each 1000 feet of elevation
   D. *increases* uniformly 3 1/2 degrees Fahrenheit for each 1000 feet of elevation

22. Generally speaking, MOST of the world's volcanoes   22.____

   A. lie in belts which are almost identical with the two great earthquake belts
   B. are roughly at right angles to the earthquake belts
   C. are in the equatorial regions
   D. form no particular geographic pattern

23. The point in the bedrock at which an earthquake seems to center is known as its   23.____

   A. anticline   B. epicenter   C. focus   D. fault

24. Of the following groups, the one which contains only metamorphic rocks is   24.____

   A. basalt, diorite, dolomite, shale
   B. conglomerate, granite, serpentine, marble
   C. diabase, schist, obsidian, serpentine
   D. quartzite, gneiss, slate, marble

25. Diastrophism refers to which one of the following? The   25.____

   A. rising and sinking of the earth's surface
   B. formation of geysers
   C. erosion caused by wind
   D. movement of clouds

26. The fraction of the solid part of the earth that lies beneath water and ice is   26.____

   A. 1/3   B. 1/2   C. 3/4   D. 5/6

27. The surface of the solid part of the earth consists essentially of huge blocks of rock which sometimes break away and rise or sink.
This action is called   27.____

   A. volcanic action   B. folding
   C. faulting   D. weathering

28. Of the following groups of materials found in the earth's crust, the group in which the items range progressively from softest to hardest is   28.____

   A. talc, fluorite, quartz, diamond
   B. feldspar, gypsum, topaz, corundum
   C. gypsum, quartz, apatite, diamond
   D. calcite, quartz, diamond, corundum

29. Which one of the following groups contains the four MOST abundant elements in the earth's crust?

29.____

   A. Oxygen, nitrogen, hydrogen, iron
   B. Nitrogen, iron, sodium, oxygen
   C. Potassium, silicon, aluminum, iron
   D. Oxygen, silicon, aluminum, iron

30. All but one of the following statements about artesian wells are true. The EXCEPTION is:

30.____

   A. Artesian well water is usually much colder than ordinary well water.
   B. The water in artesian wells is drawn from aquifers below an impervious layer.
   C. Artesian well water is usually harder than ordinary well water.
   D. The source of the water supply in an artesian well may be hundreds of miles from the well.

31. When oil spouts from a well as a gusher, it USUALLY does so because

31.____

   A. of the pressure of water beneath the oil or of gas above the oil
   B. air is pumped into the well
   C. of the release of great heat
   D. of the tremendous pressure of subsurface rock layers on the oil

32. The new volcano which was formed in Mexico in 1943 is named

32.____

   A. Popocatepetl   B. Mauna Loa
   C. Paricutin   D. Krakatoa

33. A narrow v-shaped valley is considered by geologists to be

33.____

   A. young   B. old
   C. mature   D. between mature and old

34. As compared with a valley made by a stream, a glacial valley is

34.____

   A. rounded and smooth   B. irregular and rough
   C. irregular and smooth   D. rounded and rough

35. The branch of geology dealing with the origin of land forms is called

35.____

   A. geomorphology   B. geopolitics
   C. geomology   D. geotology

36. The farthest south in what is now the continental United States of America that the last glacier reached was

36.____

   A. Maine   B. New York   C. Kentucky   D. Alabama

37. Of the following mountain ranges, the one estimated to be the YOUNGEST is the

37.___

   A. Alps   B. Rockies
   C. Adirondacks   D. Himalayas

38. About 100,000,000 years ago, North America

    A. had approximately the same form as today except that a land bridge connected Alaska and Siberia
    B. was connected by land to Asia, South America, and Europe
    C. was divided into two parts by a great inland sea
    D. was connected by a land bridge to Africa

38.____

39. Of the following epochs, the one which is NOT associated with the Mesozoic Era is the

    A. Cretaceous   B. Jurassic
    C. Triassic   D. Permian

39.____

40. The Moh Scale measures the

    A. acidity of the soil
    B. hardness of rocks
    C. bacterial content of the soil
    D. proportion of nitrogen to potash

40.____

41. A line on a weather map indicating that warm air has been lifted from the earth's surface by the action of opposing wedges of cold air is called a(n) _____ front.

    A. cold   B. warm   C. occluded   D. stationary

41.____

42. Points of equal pressure on weather maps are connected by lines called

    A. isotherms   B. isobars   C. isotopes   D. millibars

42.____

43. When contour lines on a topographical map are wide apart, it means that the area between the contour lines represents a(n)

    A. extensive lake   B. steep rise
    C. comparatively level area   D. desert

43.____

44. On a U.S. Geological Survey topographical map, the point at which contour lines meet represents a

    A. valley   B. hill   C. cliff   D. plain

44.____

45. The instrument among those named below which is used to determine latitude is the

    A. barometer   B. chronometer
    C. sextant   D. anemometer

45.____

46. The condition of *nine months of winter and three months of bad weather* in eastern Newfoundland is caused CHIEFLY by the

    A. Gulf Stream   B. Brazil Current
    C. Labrador Current   D. Sargasso Sea

46.____

47. The COMMONEST cause of hard water is the presence of compounds of

    A. fluorine   B. calcium   C. iron   D. sulfur

47.____

48. All of the following metals are extracted from the minerals with which they are associated   48.____
below EXCEPT

   A. iron from hematite   B. uranium from pitchblende
   C. tin from sphalerite   D. lead from galena

49. Iron pyrites, sometimes known as fool's gold, is mined CHIEFLY for use in the manufac-   49.____
ture of

   A. costume jewelry   B. sulfuric acid
   C. porcelain and china   D. paint

50. Of the following acids, the one MOST often used to test for calcite is cold dilute _____   50.____
acid.

   A. hydrochloric   B. carbonic
   C. sulfuric   D. nitric

KEY (CORRECT ANSWERS)

1. D	11. C	21. A	31. A	41. C
2. B	12. B	22. A	32. C	42. B
3. B	13. A	23. C	33. A	43. C
4. B	14. B	24. D	34. A	44. C
5. D	15. B	25. A	35. A	45. C
6. B	16. C	26. C	36. C	46. C
7. C	17. C	27. C	37. B	47. B
8. A	18. B	28. A	38. C	48. C
9. C	19. B	29. D	39. D	49. B
10. B	20. B	30. A	40. B	50. A

TEST 2

DIRECTIONS: Each question or incomplete statement is followed by several suggested answers or completions. Select the one that BEST answers the question or completes the statement. *PRINT THE LETTER OF THE CORRECT ANSWER IN THE SPACE AT THE RIGHT.*

1. The destructive distillation of soft coal produces

    A. coal gas, bitumen, water gas, and tar
    B. ammonia, coal gas, water gas, and coke
    C. coal tar, coal gas, ammonia, and coke
    D. coal tar, coke, ammonia, and charcoal

1.____

2. If a chemist uses air displacement in a mouth-downward container for the laboratory collection of a gas, the gas is PROBABLY _____ in water and _____ than air.

    A. insoluble; heavier
    C. soluble; heavier
    B. insoluble; lighter
    D. soluble; lighter

2.____

3. To make hydrogen as a classroom demonstration, the USUAL procedure is to use hydrochloric acid and

    A. Zn   B. Cu   C. Hg   D. Ag

3.____

4. The spontaneous disintegration of thorium is known as

    A. radioactivity   B. fission   C. fusion   D. half-life

4.____

5. The nuclear particle with mass 1 and with unit positive charge is the

    A. meson   B. positron   C. alpha particle   D. proton

5.____

6. The valence of calcium in $Ca_3(PO_4)_2$ is

    A. 1   B. 2   C. 5   D. 6

6.____

7. The MOST active of the halogens is

    A. iodine   B. fluorine   C. chlorine   D. bromine

7.____

8. Calcium oxide always contains 40 units by weight of calcium to 16 units by weight of oxygen.
This illustrates the law of

    A. mass action
    C. constant composition
    B. multiple proportions
    D. combining proportions

8.____

9. Which one of the following is a balanced equation?

    A. $HgO \rightarrow Hg + O_2$
    B. $Zn + Cl_2 \rightarrow 2ZnCl_2$
    C. $Mg + H_2SO_4 \rightarrow H_2 + MgSO_4$
    D. $FeCl_3 + KOH \rightarrow Fe(OH)_3 + KCl$

9.____

10. Which one of the following is a balanced equation?

    A. $Ca(OH)_2 + Na_2CO_3 \rightarrow CaCO_3 + 2NaOH$
    B. $PbCl_2 + H_2S \rightarrow PbS + HCl$
    C. $BaCl_2 + Na_2SO_4 \rightarrow 2BaSO_4 + NaCl$
    D. $CO + Fe_2O_3 \rightarrow CO_2 + 2Fe$

10.____

11. In the reaction between NaOH and H_2SO_4, 11._____

    A. the Na^+ is reduced   B. the $SO_4^=$ gains electrons
    C. the loses electrons   D. none of the above

12. Corn oil is changed to margarine by 12._____

    A. hydrogenation   B. hydrolysis
    C. dehydration   D. hydration

13. Which one of the following compounds does NOT contain an element common to the others? 13._____

    A. Potassium chlorate   B. Grain alcohol
    C. Hydrogen fluoride   D. Sulfurous acid

14. A noncombustible solvent for grease, the vapor of which solvent is poisonous, is 14._____

    A. H_2O B. CCl_4 C. NaOH   D. C_2H_5OH

15. Which one of the following alloys contains copper? 15._____

    A. Solder   B. Sterling silver
    C. Gold amalgam   D. Stainless steel

16. A safety device in a common hydrogen generator is a 16._____

    A. pan   B. delivery tube
    C. thistle tube   D. pneumatic trough

17. Of the following scientists, the one who developed a useful pictorial representation of the atom is 17._____

    A Bohr   B. DcBroglie
    C. Heisenberg   D. Schrodinger

18. Which one of the following procedures is used to speed up the reaction between iron and hydrochloric acid? 18._____

    A. Exposing the reagents to bright light
    B. Keeping the reagents cool
    C. Heating the reagents
    D. Filtering the hydrochloric acid

19. Which one of the following is an example of double replacement? 19._____

    A. $C + CO_2 \rightarrow 2CO$

    B. $KOH + HCl \rightarrow HOH + KCl$

    C. $2AgNO_3 + Cu \rightarrow Cu(NO_3)_2 + 2Ag$

    D. $SO_2 + \frac{1}{2}O_2 \rightarrow SO_3$

20. The action of aqua regia on metals converts them to   20.____

    A. nitrates   B. sulfates   C. chlorides   D. sulfides

21. When a hot saturated solution of copper sulfate cools,   21.____

    A. copper will separate
    B. nothing will happen
    C. a white solid forms
    D. blue crystals are produced

22. Given the atomic weight of aluminum as 27 and the atomic weight of chlorine as 35.5,   22.____
    the molecular weight of aluminum chloride is

    A. 62.5   B. 98
    C. 133.5   D. none of the above

23. The molecular weight of sucrose, $C_{12}H_{22}O_{11}$, (Atomic weights: C = 12, H = 1, O = 16), is   23.____

    A. 1   B. 45   C. 159   D. 342

24. The percent of carbon dioxide in the air is CLOSEST to which one of the following?   24.____

    A. 1%   B. .03%   C. 20%   D. 78%

25. When the molecular equation showing the reaction between Al and HCl is balanced, the   25.____
    coefficient before the HCl is

    A. 1 understood   B. 2
    C. 4   D. 6

26. Moore and Ross recently ascended to a height of 80,000 ft. and discovered   26.____

    A. cosmic ray bombardment from space
    B. the nature of the rings of Saturn
    C. water vapor in the atmosphere of Venus
    D. new values for the space unit, Mach

27. A reaction that goes to completion is illustrated by   27.____

    A. $KCl + I_2 \rightarrow$ B. $CuSO_4 + HCl \rightarrow$
    C. $Na_2SO_3 + H_2O \rightarrow$ D. $NaHCO_3 + H_2SO_4 \rightarrow$

28. Metallic sodium and chlorine are products of the electrolysis of which one of the follow-   28.____
    ing?

    A. Brine
    B. Sodium hypochlorite solution
    C. Sodium chlorate solution
    D. Molten sodium chloride

29. From 54 grams of water, one can extract how many grams of hydrogen?   29.____
   A. 1   B. 2   C. 6   D. 16

30. Which one of the following is a laboratory source of SO_2?   30.____
   A. Na_2SO_3 B. Na_2SO_4 C. Na_2S D. $NaHSO_4$

31. Which one of the following substances is used in transistors?   31.____
   A. Radium   B. Uranium   C. Germanium   D. Thorium

32. The gram molecular weight of water is   32.____
   A. 1   B. 2   C. 3   D. 18

33. Ammonia is produced by the _____ process.   33.____
   A. Solvay   B. Frasch   C. Haber   D. Flotation

34. Which one of the following substances may be used to test for proteins?   34.____
   A. $Ca(OH)_2$ B. HNO_3 C. $CuSO_4$ D. $Al(NO_3)_2$

35. The LIGHTEST of the following types of sodium particles is a(n)   35.____
   A. atom   B. molecule   C. crystal   D. ion

36. At standard pressure, 83 grams of an undissociated solute, dissolved in a 1000g. of   36.____
   water, elevates the boiling point $1.04°$ C.
   The gram-molecular weight of the solute is
   A. 41.5   B. 83   C. 86.32   D. 166

37. A science teacher wishes to demonstrate chemical change by the reaction between Fe   37.____
   and S, atomic weights 56 and 32, respectively.
   The weight of sulfur which should be reacted with 2 grams of iron is CLOSEST to
   which one of the following?
   A. 0.5   B. 1.5   C. 3   D. 4

38. Of the following raw materials, the one MOST important in the chemical industry is   38.____
   A. NaCl   B. H_2SO_4 C. $NaHCO_3$ D. Na_2CO_3

39. Water is MOST readily decomposed by which one of the following?   39.____
   A. Iron   B. Potassium   C. Magnesium   D. Calcium

40. The INCORRECT pair of items in the following couplets of compound and commercial   40.____
   use is
   A. $CHCl_3$ solvent   B. $COCl_2$ water purification
   C. $CaOCl_2$ bleaching   D. NaCl manufacture of HCl

41. Of the following, an example of a fully oxidized non-combustible substance is

    A. C_3H_8 B. CCl_4 C. CH_3Cl D. C_2H_5OH

41.____

42. Which one of the following is the formula for a hydrocarbon?

    A. $C_6H_{10}O_5$ B. $CHCl_3$ C. C_3H_8 D. $A_2C_2O_4$

42.____

43. The E.M.F. required to maintain an electrolysis

    A. is independent of the products
    B. is the same for all ionic substances in equal concentration
    C. is related to the decomposition potential
    D. depends upon the source of the E.M.F.

43.____

44. The Minuteman guided missile is different from the Atlas and the Titan that preceded it in that the Minuteman

    A. is a tactical weapon of limited range
    B. is jet powered
    C. requires high altitude launching
    D. is powered by solid fuel

44.____

45. If a gram-molecular volume of an unknown gas weighs 320 grams, its relative molecular weight is

    A. 10   B. 20   C. 160   D. 320

45.____

46. When a splint which has been burning in a bottle of air goes out, the residue gas contains

    A. no oxygen   B. only carbon dioxide
    C. some oxygen   D. only nitrogen

46.____

47. In the United States, a research program recently developed extremely lightweight thermoelectric generators using

    A. boiling heavy water reactors
    B. principles of steam regeneration
    C. thermocouples
    D. high energy linear accelerators

47.____

48. The reaction between nitrogen and hydrogen is promoted by the addition of pressure to the system.
This is BEST explained by _____ Law.

    A. LeChatelier's   B. Dumas'   C. Dalton's   D. Charles

48.____

49. In the Laue method of determination of crystal structure, the crystal is bombarded with

    A. neutrons   B. protons   C. x-rays   D. alpha particles

49.____

50. The percentage composition of an oxide of iron is approximately 72.4 for iron and 27.6 for oxygen. Given atomic weights Fe = 56 and O = 16, the formula for the compound is

    A. FeO B. Fe_2O_3 C. Fe_3O_4 D. $Fe_2O_3 \cdot Fe_3O_4$

50.____

KEY (CORRECT ANSWERS)

1.	C	11.	D	21.	D	31.	C	41.	B
2.	D	12.	A	22.	C	32.	D	42.	C
3.	A	13.	C	23.	D	33.	C	43.	C
4.	A	14.	B	24.	B	34.	B	44.	D
5.	D	15.	B	25.	D	35.	D	45.	D
6.	B	16.	C	26.	C	36.	A	46.	C
7.	B	17.	A	27.	D	37.	B	47.	C
8.	C	18.	C	28.	D	38.	A	48.	A
9.	C	19.	B	29.	C	39.	B	49.	C
10.	A	20.	C	30.	A	40.	B	50.	C

TEST 3

DIRECTIONS: Each question or incomplete statement is followed by several suggested answers or completions. Select the one that BEST answers the question or completes the statement. *PRINT THE LETTER OF THE CORRECT ANSWER IN THE SPACE AT THE RIGHT.*

1. Differentiation in structure to adapt to special function is illustrated by   1._____

    A. jaw and teeth of sharks
    B. beaks of birds
    C. tooth structure of mammals
    D. all of the above

2. Which one of the following terms includes all the others?   2._____

    A. Organ   B. Organism   C. Cell   D. Tissue

3. The cell membrane is permeable to all of the following EXCEPT   3._____

    A. sugar   B. starch   C. oxygen   D. salt

4. Sugar solution is distributed in a plant through which one of the following?   4._____

    A. Bast fibers   B. Xylem
    C. Sieve tubes   D. Wood ducts

5. Which one of the following processes stores energy?   5._____

    A. Assimilation   B. Respiration
    C. Metabolism   D. Photosynthesis

6. Which of the following is a factor CHIEFLY responsible for the rise of sap in trees during the summer?   6._____

    A. Root pressure   B. Transpiration
    C. Adhesion   D. Diffusion

7. Leguminous plants, such as vetch, are planted MAINLY to achieve which one of the following?   7._____

    A. Bind the soil   B. Conserve soil water
    C. Add soil nitrates   D. Prevent soil erosion

8. The gametophyte generation is the dominant one in MOST   8._____

    A. bryophytes   B. ferns
    C. grasses   D. flowering plants

9. The mapping of chromosomes has been made possible LARGELY through careful study of   9._____

    A. Mendel's Laws
    B. crossover percentage between linked genes
    C. ploidy
    D. mutation

10. The crucial point in animal mitosis is the division of the   10.____

    A. cell into two parts
    B. chromosomes so that each daughter cell receives a full set of chromosomes
    C. cytoplasm so that each daughter cell receives an equal amount
    D. centriole into two equal parts

11. In the development of the animal embryo, the sequence is fertilization,   11.____

    A. cleavage, blastula, invagination, gastrula
    B. blastula; cleavage, gastrule, invagination
    C. gastrula, cleavage, invagination, blastula
    D. cleavage, invagination, blastula, gastrula

12. Chordate embryos, in their development, follow a regular pattern in which distinctions   12.____
among

    A. classes appear first
    B. orders appear first
    C. species appear first
    D. different chordates are not discernible

13. Among the following, the structure LEAST closely related to the others is   13.____

    A. flipper of porpoise   B. fin of shark
    C. wing of bird   D. wing of bat

14. Joshua Lederburg received a Nobel Prize for his work in   14.____

    A. bacterial genetics   B. virus transmutation
    C. origin of virus   D. bacteriophage

15. The MOST important function accomplished by meiosis is the   15.____

    A. formation of a variety of haploid gametes
    B. splitting of chromosomes into two equal parts
    C. formation of polar bodies
    D. formation of identical gametes

16. An omnivorous food habit would MOST likely be associated with which one of the follow-   16.____
ing?

    A. Relatively unspecialized tooth structure
    B. Well-developed incisors
    C. Well-developed canines
    D. Well-developed molars

17. The energy yield of food is measured by   17.____

    A. a thermometer   B. a thermocouple
    C. calorimeter   D. B.T.U.'s

18. The PRINCIPAL nutrient constituent of the human body, by weight, is   18.____

    A. minerals   B. fat   C. protein   D. water

19. The ULTIMATE source of food in the sea is   19.____

    A. plankton   B. shell fish
    C. marine worms   D. small teleosts

20. Which one of the following is NOT a protein?   20.____

    A. Gluten   B. Hemoglobin   C. Chlorophyll   D. Glycogen

21. Food is moved through the alimentary canal CHIEFLY by   21.____

    A. muscular spasms   B. peristalsis
    C. sphincter muscles   D. voluntary muscles

22. Which one of the following is NOT a product of digestion?   22.____

    A. Glycogen   B. Fatty acids   C. Amino acids   D. Glucose

23. All of the following enzymes help to digest carbohydrates EXCEPT   23.____

    A. amylase   B. lipase   C. maltase   D. ptyalin

24. Basal metabolism is   24.____

    A. metabolic rate for minimal activity
    B. average metabolic rate
    C. metabolic rate for normal activity
    D. metabolic rate of a newborn infant

25. Each of the following is at least in part an endocrine gland EXCEPT the   25.____

    A. pancreas   B. ovary   C. pituitary   D. liver

26. Each of the following is necessary for normal blood function EXCEPT   26.____

    A. alpha-naphtha quinone   B. alphatocopherol
    C. folic acid   D. vitamin B_{12}

27. Red corpuscles are formed in   27.____

    A. bone marrow   B. lymph node   C. liver   D. blood

28. Lacteals are   28.____

    A. milk glands   B. lymph capillaries
    C. lymph glands   D. blood capillaries

29. Blood does NOT distribute oxygen in which one of the following?   29.____

    A. Frog   B. Grasshopper   C. Whale   D. Starfish

30. The MOST effective of the following methods of increasing the respiratory rate is to   30.____
    _____ in the inspired air.

    A. *increase* the amount of oxygen
    B. *decrease* the amount of oxygen
    C. *increase* the amount of carbon dioxide
    D. *decrease* the amount of carbon dioxide

31. Membranous walls, rich blood supply, and large surface area are characteristic of the 31.____

    A. kidney   B. lung
    C. small intestine   D. all of the above

32. Of the following statements about the process known as photosynthesis, the one which 32.____
    is INCORRECT is:

    A. Nitrogen is a by-product of the process.
    B. Chlorophyll and sunlight are necessary for it to take place.
    C. It takes place most rapidly in temperatures from 80-90° F.
    D. A carbohydrate is the end result of the process.

33. The MOST common type of non-nucleated cell in the human body is the _____ cell. 33.____

    A. red blood   B. white blood
    C. epithelial   D. nerve

34. The energy for muscular contraction results from the breakdown of 34.____

    A. ATP   B. ACTH   C. DNA   D. PAS

35. In animals, the problem of providing a fluid medium in which the sperm may reach the 35.____
    egg is solved by

    A. liberating both eggs and sperm in water with subsequent external fertilization and
       development
    B. liberating sperm in water with subsequent external fertilization and development
    C. liberating sperm directly into the body of the female with subsequent internal fertili-
       zation and development
    D. all of the above

36. The act of restoring a lost part by growing a new one is called 36.____

    A. asexual reproduction   B. regeneration
    C. growth   D. parthenogenesis

37. In the binomial system of nomenclature, each living thing is named by 37.____

    A. class and species   B. class and order
    C. order and family   D. genus and species

38. Chordates are characterized by 38.____

    A. notochord and dorsal hollow nerve cord
    B. notochord and ventral nerve cord
    C. bilateral symmetry and four-chambered heart
    D. bilateral symmetry and three-chambered heart

39. The classic experiment on spontaneous generation was performed by 39.____

    A. Aristotle   B. Hooke   C. Brown   D. Redi

40. *Study nature, not books* was the advice of   40.____

    A. Linnaeus   B. Darwin   C. Agassiz   D. Leeuwenhoek

41. Which one of the following items includes the others?   41.____

    A. Visual purple   B. Rods and cones
    C. Fovea   D. Retina

42. Functional damage to the brain may be studied by the use of which one of the following?   42.____

    A. X-rays   B. Electrocardiograph
    C. Electroencephalograph   D. Radioisotopes

43. Which one of the following organs is NOT concerned with the elimination of metabolic   43.____
waste from the human body?

    A. Lungs   B. Kidneys   C. Skin   D. Spleen

44. Which one of the following is used as a test for acid ions?   44.____

    A. Eosine   B. Brom thymol blue
    C. Indophenol   D. Hyposulphite of soda

45. Penicillin was discovered by   45.____

    A. Florey   B. Ehrlich   C. Fleming   D. Waksman

46. Which one of the following animals is used in making Salk vaccine?   46.____

    A. Chick embryos B. Rabbits   C. Monkeys   D. Horses

47. It is generally believed that a sore throat which has been diagnosed as diphtheria should   47.____
be immediately treated with

    A. toxoid   B. toxin-antitoxin
    C. streptomycin   D. antitoxin

48. Which one of the following was the last and MOST important development in the   48.____
1950's war on polio?

    A. Large scale testing of an orally administered vaccine containing live polio virus
    B. Large scale testing of an orally administered vaccine containing dead polio virus
    C. Injection of a vaccine containing live polio virus
    D. Injection of a vaccine containing dead polio virus

49. An important indicator of the degree of cumulative action of radioactive fall-out is the   49.____
measurement of the amount of

    A. iodine 131 in thyroid tissue
    B. strontium 90 in bone tissue
    C. carbon 14 in epithelial tissue
    D. phosphorus 30 in tooth enamel

50. Which one of the following has been saved from extinction by conservation measures?   50.____

    A. Passenger pigeon   B. Egret
    C. Heath hen   D. Labrador duck

KEY (CORRECT ANSWERS)

1. D	11. A	21. B	31. D	41. D
2. B	12. A	22. A	32. A	42. C
3. B	13. B	23. B	33. A	43. D
4. C	14. A	24. A	34. A	44. B
5. D	15. D	25. D	35. D	45. C
6. B	16. A	26. B	36. B	46. C
7. C	17. C	27. A	37. D	47. D
8. A	18. D	28. B	38. A	48. A
9. B	19. A	29. B	39. D	49. B
10. B	20. D	30. C	40. C	50. B

TEST 4

1. Pressure in a gas is explained by which one of the following?   1.____

   A. The kinetic theory of gases
   B. The Brownian movement
   C. Mariotte's contribution to Boyle's Law
   D. Charles' Law

2. What horizontal force is required to pull a 10 lb. loaded wooden box on a level glass plate   2.____
   when the coefficient of sliding friction between glass and wood is 0.15?
   _____ lb.(s).

   A. 1.5   B. 6.67   C. 9.85   D. 15

3. The absolute unit of force required to accelerate one pound of mass at the rate of one   3.____
   foot per second is the

   A. dyne   B. momentum   C. poundal   D. slug

4. The E.M.F. generated in a conductor when it is moved across magnetic lines of force   4.____
   depends upon

   A. strength of the field   B. length of the conductor
   C. speed of the conductor   D. all of the above

5. A ten pound ball is swung around on the end of a 5 ft. nylon cord.   5.____
   If the velocity of the ball is 20 feet per second, what is the centrifugal force in pounds?
   _____ lb(s).

   A. 1   B. 1.32   C. 25   D. 200

6. The period of a pendulum is independent of which one of the following?   6.____

   A. Length of the pendulum
   B. Arc through which the pendulum swings
   C. Acceleration due to gravity
   D. Material and mass of the pendulum

7. Where MUST the object be placed in front of a spherical concave mirror in order that the   7.____
   image be magnified?

   A. At the principal focus
   B. Beyond the center of curvature
   C. At the center of curvature
   D. Between the principal focus and the mirror

8. Spherical aberration in a camera lens can be reduced to a MINIMUM by using a   8.____

   A. color filter   B. Polaroid filter
   C. small diaphragm opening   D. large diaphragm opening

9. Chromatic aberration is USUALLY corrected by   9.____

   A. a double concave lens
   B. a Polaroid lens
   C. a color filter
   D. cementing a converging lens into a compound lens

10. Astigmatism may be corrected by a _____ lens.   10.____

    A. bifocal   B. spherical
    C. cylindrical   D. compound

11. The primary colors of light are   11.____

    A. red, blue, and green
    B. magenta, blue-green, and yellow
    C. red, blue, and yellow
    D. red, orange, yellow, green, blue, and violet

12. When white light is passed through a prism, the color of light that is bent the MOST is   12.____

    A. red   B. yellow   C. green   D. violet

13. Two colors of light which together produce white light are called   13.____

    A. primary light colors   B. complementary colors
    C. additives   D. neutrals

14. The spectrum of the sun is BEST called a _____ spectrum.   14.____

    A. continuous   B. bright line
    C. absorption   D. Frauhofer

15. When white light is passed through a prism, the lights of different colors are separated because of   15.____

    A. interference   B. scattering
    C. dispersion   D. polarization

16. The quantum theory of light was proposed by   16.____

    A. Einstein   B. Newton   C. Planck   D. Huyghens

17. In an A.C. series circuit, the resistance is 40 ohms, inductive reactance is 50 ohms, the capacitative reactance is 20 ohms.   17.____
    What is the TOTAL impedance?
    _____ ohms.

    A. 50   B. 70   C. 75   D. 110

18. Three resistances of 20, 30, and 60 ohms are connected in parallel to a 120 volt source.   18.____
    The TOTAL resistance of the group is _____ ohms.

    A. 10   B. 110   C. 36.7   D. 40

19. The voltage across a lamp is 10 volts. The current is 2 amperes.   19.____
    What is the resistance in ohms? _____ ohms.

    A. 0.2   B. 2.5   C. 5   D. 20

20. The maximum voltage in an A.C. circuit is 140 volts. The effective voltage is CLOSEST to   20.____
    which one of the following?
    _____ volts.

    A. 70   B. 98.98   C. 93.33   D. 110

21. Of the following statements, the one that is NOT true is that, in general,   21.____

    A. dense gases are better transmitters of sound waves than rare gases
    B. liquids are better transmitters of sound waves than solids
    C. liquids are better transmitters of sound waves than gases
    D. solids are better transmitters of sound waves than gases

22. Of the following statements, the one which is TRUE is: Sound   22.____

    A. is the result of electrons passing through a magnetic field
    B. is the result of atomic vibrations within the molecule
    C. results when a string is vibrated in a vacuum
    D. results from a series of forward and backward movements of molecules of air

23. Which one of the following statements is TRUE? The _____ loudspeaker.   23.____

    A. tweeter is a high frequency
    B. woofer is a treble
    C. tweeter is a bass
    D. woofer is a high frequency

24. The ratio between the friction experienced by an airplane moving at 600 miles per hour   24.____
    and that experienced by an airplane moving 300 miles per hour, other things being
    equal, is

    A. 1:1   B. 2:1   C. 3:1   D. 4:1

25. In long distance transmission of electrical power, the line losses are reduced by   25.____

    A. high amperage and low voltage
    B. low amperage and high voltage
    C. high towers
    D. high amperage and high voltage

26. Television broadcasting uses   26.____

    A. ultra high frequency waves, a channel width of 6 megacycles, and transmits an
        audio, video, and synchronizing signal
    B. high frequency waves, a channel width of 4.5 megacycles and two transmitters
    C. radio waves, a channel width of 6 megacycles and AM and FM signal transmission
    D. ultra high frequency waves, a channel width of 4.5 megacycles, and transmits an
        audio and video signal

27. In a television receiver, the kinescope is ESSENTIALLY a(n)   27.____

    A. cathode ray oscilloscope   B. image orthicon
    C. iconoscope   D. photo cathode

28. The color TV system adopted by the Federal Communications Commission operates 28.____
with

    A. 525 line interlaced scanning and picture frequency of 30 cycles per second
    B. 262 1/2 line scanning and picture frequency of 60 cycles per second
    C. 525 line scanning and picture frequency of 60 cycles per second
    D. 265 1/2 line scanning and picture frequency of 30 cycles per second

29. The operation of rocket engines is possible because of the law of 29.____

    A. conservation of energy   B. conservation of momentum
    C. gravity   D. Corolis force

30. The *escape velocity* for the earth is CLOSEST to which one of the following? 30.____

    A. Seven miles a minute   B. 5,000 miles per hour
    C. 25,000 miles per hour   D. 186,000 miles per hour

31. Isotopes are elements of 31.____

    A. same atomic number but different atomic weights
    B. same atomic weight but different atomic number
    C. same number of planetary electrons and the same atomic weight
    D. different number of planetary electrons and different numbers of neutrons in their
       nuclei

32. Radioactive elements, such as radium and uranium, are spontaneously disintegrating 32.____
and emitting particles including

    A. helium nuclei, electrons, and x-rays
    B. helium ions, neutrons, and deuterons
    C. helium nuclei, electrons, and positrons
    D. electrons, x-rays, and photons

33. The amount of energy lost per mass unit particle when the protons and neutrons are 33.____
packed together in the nucleus of an atom is called

    A. nuclear energy   B. the packing factor
    C. the energy level   D. thermonuclear energy

34. When a liquid expands as it freezes, the solid formed will, if kept in the original liquid at 34.____
the freezing temperature,

    A. float   B. melt   C. dissolve   D. sink

35. The electrical unit which equals 6.25×10^{18} electrons is called the 35.____

    A. ampere   B. volt   C. coulomb   D. farad

36. The torque exerted on a bar magnet of pole strength m and length 1, placed perpendicu- 36.____
larly to a magnetic field of intensity H, is

    A. $\dfrac{Hm}{l^2}$ B. Hml C. $\dfrac{H+m}{l^2}$ D. $\dfrac{\sqrt{H^2+m^2}}{l^2}$

37. Of the following, the BEST approximation for the angle of magnetic declination in New York City is

    A. 12° W   B. 12° E   C. 75° W   D. 43° N

37.____

38. An induced current in a coil has such a direction that it produces a magnetic field which opposes the motion of the magnetic field by which the current is produced.
This is known as

    A. Lenz's Law   B. Oersted's Discovery
    C. Faraday's Law   D. D'Arsonval's Principle

38.____

39. The compound microscope was invented by

    A. Van Leeuwenhoek   B. Huyghens
    C. Newton   D. Galileo

39.____

40. The density of water is

    A. maximum at 4° C

    B. maximum at 0° C

    C. maximum at -4° C

    D. independent of the temperature

40.____

41. The fuel mixture is ALWAYS ignited by the heat of compression in the _____ engine.

    A. two-stroke gasoline

    B. multiple cylindered gasoline

    C. diesel

    D. gas turbine

41.____

42. The operating frequency of a broadcasting station whose assigned wavelength is 250 meters is

    A. 12,000 cycles   B. 1200 kilocycles
    C. 12,000,000 cycles   D. 12 megacycles

42.____

43. The BEST radiator of heat is a _____ surface.

    A. rough, black   B. smooth, black
    C. rough, silvered   D. smooth, silvered

43.____

44. In a deep lake, the water at the bottom of the lake rarely falls below what Centigrade temperature?

    A. 0   B. 4   C. 32   D. 100

44.____

45. The temperature of water boiling in a pressure cooker in New York City is MOST likely to be closest to

    A. 100° C   B. 98.6° C   C. 80° C   D. 110° C

45.____

46. The specific heat of iron is 0.11.
The number of calories required to raise the temperature of 10 grams of iron from 20° C to 30° C is

    A. 10   B. 11
    C. 110   D. none of the above

46.____

47. Of the following, the metals which make an alloy used for very strong permanent magnets is   47.____

    A. iron, nickel, and sulfur
    B. tempered steel and silicon
    C. carefully purified iron and molybdenum
    D. cobalt, aluminum, and nickel

48. On a map of terrestrial magnetism, the line joining all points where a compass needle points true north is called the   48.____

    A. aclinic   B. isoclinic   C. isogonic   D. agonic

49. If both ends of a piece of steel strongly repel the south pole of a compass, we may conclude that   49.____

    A. the steel bar is not a magnet
    B. each of the two ends is a south pole
    C. the steel bar is paramagnetic
    D. the phenomenon is caused by magnetic induction

50. If a magnetic pole of 10 emu is repelled with a force of 8 dynes by a second magnetic pole 5 cm. away, the strength of the second magnetic pole is _____ emu.   50.____

    A. 20   B. 30   C. 40   D. 190

KEY (CORRECT ANSWERS)

1.	A	11.	A	21.	B	31.	A	41.	C
2.	A	12.	D	22.	D	32.	A	42.	B
3.	C	13.	B	23.	A	33.	B	43.	A
4.	D	14.	C	24.	D	34.	A	44.	B
5.	C	15.	C	25.	B	35.	C	45.	D
6.	D	16.	C	26.	A	36.	B	46.	B
7.	D	17.	A	27.	A	37.	A	47.	D
8.	C	18.	A	28.	A	38.	A	48.	D
9.	D	19.	C	29.	B	39.	D	49.	B
10.	C	20.	B	30.	C	40.	A	50.	A

EXAMINATION SECTION
TEST 1

DIRECTIONS: Each question or incomplete statement is followed by several suggested answers or completions. Select the one that BEST answers the question or completes the statement. *PRINT THE LETTER OF THE CORRECT ANSWER IN THE SPACE AT THE RIGHT.*

1. Respiration in plants occurs   1.____

    A. only on cloudy days   B. only in the night
    C. only in the daytime   D. all the time

2. The complex chemical ATP is necessary to produce   2.____

    A. fats   B. sugars
    C. proteins   D. amino acids

3. A medicine obtained from the bark of the cinchona tree is   3.____

    A. atabrine   B. pentaquine
    C. chloroquine   D. quinine

4. A radioactive element used to study photosynthesis in green plants is   4.____

    A. I^{131} B. C^{14} C. N^{16} D. U^{233}

5. The selectivity of a cell depends upon the   5.____

    A. cell membrane   B. nucleus
    C. cytoplasm   D. mitochondria

6. The zoologist who helped formulate the cell theory was   6.____

    A. Schleiden   B. Hooke   C. Purkinje   D. Schwann

7. The brown spots on the back of fern fronds produce   7.____

    A. pollen   B. spores   C. scales   D. seeds

8. Plants without true roots, stems, or leaves are called   8.____

    A. bryophytes   B. spermatophytes
    C. thallophytes   D. pteridophytes

9. Of the following, the CLOSEST biological relative of the whale is the   9.____

    A. shark   B. toad   C. crocodile   D. horse

10. The process LEAST likely to result in vitamin loss is   10.____

    A. bleaching celery   B. refining flour
    C. quick freezing fruits   D. peeling vegetables

11. A trait determined by two identical alleles is said to be   11.____

    A. homologous   B. analogous
    C. heterozygous   D. homozygous

12. The nutrient that produces the LARGEST number of calories per gram of weight is   12._____

    A. protein   B. starch   C. carbohydrate   D. fat

13. A method used to condition the soil by spreading straw, manure, or peat moss over it is   13._____

    A. fallowing   B. terracing   C. leaching   D. mulching

14. The plant that acts as an alternate host for the wheat rust is   14._____

    A. gooseberry   B. white pine
    C. red cedar   D. barberry

15. In the process of respiration in a plant,   15._____

    A. potential energy is stored
    B. chlorophyll is necessary
    C. stored food is utilized
    D. protein is synthesized

16. The insect that feeds on the cottony cushion scale is the   16._____

    A. Ladybird bettle   B. Boll weevil
    C. Tachina fly   D. Hessian fly

17. Food made in the leaves moves to all parts of a green plant through the   17._____

    A. stomates   B. phloem   C. pith   D. xylem

18. Deamination of proteins occurs MAINLY in the   18._____

    A. small intestine   B. liver
    C. spleen   D. pancreas

19. The chemical that plays a part in the passage of nerve impulses across the space between two connecting neurons is   19._____

    A. auxin   B. colchicine
    C. reserpine   D. acetylcholine

20. The gathering of white blood cells around bacteria is an example of   20._____

    A. thigmotropism   B. chemotropism
    C. geotropism   D. hydrotropism

21. The Islets of Langerhans are located in the   21._____

    A. testis   B. pancreas   C. pituitary   D. thyroid

22. The adrenal cortex is stimulated to secrete cortisone by   22._____

    A. ATP   B. ACTH   C. 2, 4-D   D. PAS

23. Liquid wastes are carried from the kidneys to the urinary bladder by the   23._____

    A. ureters   B. urethras
    C. oviducts   D. Fallopian tubes

24. The part of the brain that controls the breathing rate is the

    A. medulla   B. cerebrum
    C. cerebellum   D. hypothalamus

24.____

25. The chemicals that cause clumping of the erythrocytes in the blood are

    A. platelets   B. red corpuscles
    C. white corpuscles   D. plasma

25.____

26. An organism with an *open circuit* system of circulation is the

    A. frog   B. earthworm   C. crayfish   D. fish

26.____

27. The heart chamber that pumps blood to the aorta is the

    A. right auricle   B. right ventricle
    C. left auricle   D. left ventricle

27.____

28. The substances that are absorbed into the lacteals of the villi are

    A. amino acids   B. vitamins
    C. simple sugars   D. fatty acids

28.____

29. A chemical that has been used with great success in the treatment of tuberculosis is

    A. isoniazid   B. chloromycetin
    C. sulfanilamide   D. radioactive phosphorus

29.____

30. Ringworm disease is caused by a

    A. lichen   B. roundworm
    C. segmented worm   D. fungus

30.____

31. The organism that causes typhus fever is a(n)

    A. fungus   B. Rickettsia   C. bacterium   D. virus

31.____

32. Emotional behavior is controlled in the

    A. hypothalamus   B. cerebrum
    C. cerebellum   D. medulla

32.____

33. In a given sample of blood, clumping occurred with both A serum and B serum. The blood type was

    A. A   B. B   C. O   D. AB

33.____

34. Of the following vitamins, the one that does NOT aid in cellular oxidation is

    A. thiamin   B. niacin
    C. ascorbic acid   D. riboflavin

34.____

35. The cyton of a motor neuron is found in the

    A. posterior root ganglion
    B. anterior root ganglion
    C. gray matter of the spinal cord
    D. white matter of the spinal cord

35.____

36. An instrument that records the electrical impulses developed in the brain is the   36._____

     A. kymograph   B. electrocardiograph
     C. polygraph   D. electroencephalograph

37. The relationship between clover plants and nitrogen-fixing bacteria is a form of   37._____

     A. parasitism   B. saprophytism
     C. commensalism   D. symbiosis

38. The number of pairs of cranial nerves in man is   38._____

     A. 12   B. 31   C. 48   D. 206

39. Water pollination occurs in the   39._____

     A. water lily   B. corn
     C. spruce   D. duckweed

40. A vegetative structure that consists of an underground stem surrounded by storage-leaves is a   40._____

     A. slip   B. rhizome   C. bulb   D. tuber

41. If a planarium is cut in half, each part will grow eventually into a complete organism. This process of forming a new organism is called   41._____

     A. conjugation   B. parthenogenesis
     C. meiosis   D. regeneration

42. Passive immunity GENERALLY lasts a   42._____

     A. few weeks   B. few months
     C. few years   D. lifetime

43. Septic tanks are used in waste disposal to   43._____

     A. break down solid wastes   B. dilute sewage
     C. aerate sewage   D. filter sewage

44. The development of the polio vaccine was made possible, in part, by the discovery that the polio viruses could be cultured in test tubes on one of the following organs of Old World monkeys: 44._____

     A. Liver   B. Thyroid gland
     C. Kidney   D. Lung

45. The scientist who discovered streptomycin was   45._____

     A. Enders   B. Fleming   C. Florey   D. Waksman

46. A sex-linked disease in man is   46._____

     A. leukemia   B. anemia
     C. hemophilia.   D. erythroblastosis fetalis

47. Destruction of the red blood cells of a developing embryo may occur when the embryo is Rh _____ and the mother is Rh _____.   47.____

 A. positive; positive   B. positive; n egative
 C. negative; negative   D. negative; positive

48. The scientist who FIRST used the word mutation to describe changes that he found in the evening primrose plant was   48.____

 A. Morgan   B. Muller   C. DeVries   D. Mendel

49. The study of the functioning of living organisms is called   49.____

 A. anatomy   B. pathology   C. ecology   D. physiology

50. The fact that a white guinea pig resulted from a cross between two hybrid black guinea pigs illustrates the law of   50.____

 A. segregation   B. dominance
 C. linkage   D. independent assortment

KEY (CORRECT ANSWERS)

1. D	11. D	21. B	31. B	41. D
2. B	12. D	22. B	32. A	42. A
3. D	13. D	23. A	33. D	43. A
4. B	14. D	24. A	34. C	44. C
5. A	15. C	25. D	35. C	45. D
6. D	16. A	26. C	36. D	46. C
7. B	17. B	27. D	37. D	47. B
8. C	18. B	28. D	38. A	48. C
9. D	19. D	29. A	39. D	49. D
10. C	20. B	30. D	40. C	50. A

TEST 2

DIRECTIONS: Each question or incomplete statement is followed by several suggested answers or completions. Select the one that BEST answers the question or completes the statement. *PRINT THE LETTER OF THE CORRECT ANSWER IN THE SPACE AT THE RIGHT.*

1. When a blue Andalusian rooster is crossed with a blue Andalusian hen, the phenotypic ratio expected among the offspring will be   1.____

    A. 100% blue
    B. 50% black and 50% white
    C. 75% black and 25% white
    D. 25% white, 25% black, 50% blue

2. A vitamin that contains cobalt as part of its chemical structure is vitamin   2.____

    A. A   B. B_2 C. B_{12} D. C

3. The two-layered cup stage that forms during cleavage is called the   3.____

    A. morula   B. gastrula   C. blastula   D. mesoderm

4. The one term that includes all the others is   4.____

    A. equational division   B. gamete
    C. maturation   D. reduction division

5. Organizers are chemicals that influence   5.____

    A. differentiation   B. mitosis
    C. fertilization   D. maturation

6. The developing embryo of a mammal is protected by a liquid-filled sac called the   6.____

    A. placenta   B. amnion   C. uterus   D. allantois

7. The seedless orange is propagated by   7.____

    A. self-pollination   B. cross-pollination
    C. hybridization   D. grafting

8. One similarity between reflexes and habits is that they are BOTH   8.____

    A. inborn acts   B. autonomic acts
    C. learned acts   D. automatic

9. The MOST ancient of the following prehistoric men is   9.____

    A. Heidelberg   B. Neanderthal
    C. Pithecantropus   D. Cro-Magnon

10. The theory of *Use and Disuse* was developed by   10.____

    A. Weismann   B. Darwin   C. Wallace   D. Lamarck

11. The micturating membrane in man is an example of a(n)   11.____

    A. mutation   B. vestigial structure
    C. malformation   D. embryonic structure

12. The LATEST of the geological eras is called the   12.____

    A. cenozoic   B. paleozoic
    C. proterozoic   D. mesozoic

13. Liquids are transported through stems and roots by the   13.____

    A. epidermis   B. cortex
    C. vascular bundles   D. pith

14. An animal that is PROBABLY a link between the fish and amphibia is the   14.____

    A. archeopteryx   B. coelacanth
    C. trilobite   D. lamprey

15. The hormone that stimulates the change of glycogen to glucose in the liver is   15.____

    A. insulin   B. progestin   C. cortin   D. adrenin

16. The haploid chromosome number in the fruit fly, Drosophila, is   16.____

    A. 4   B. 8   C. 24   D. 48

17. The plant in which seed dispersal by animals occurs is the   17.____

    A. cherry   B. coconut
    C. witch hazel   D. milkweed

18. Blood tissue differentiates from the primary germ layer known as the   18.____

    A. endoderm   B. endosperm   C. mesoderm   D. ectoderm

19. Of the following types of tissue, the one which is NOT classified as connective tissue is   19.____

    A. blood   B. bone   C. cartilage   D. tendon

20. A chrysalis is a   20.____

    A. pupa case   B. nymph   C. larva   D. cocoon

21. The one term that includes all the others is _____ plant.   21.____

    A. herbaceous   B. flowering
    C. spermatophyte   D. annual

22. Nitrogen from the air is made available to plants by   22.____

    A. decay   B. fixation
    C. denitrification   D. nitrate bacteria

23. The series of muscular waves of contraction in the alimentary canal is called   23.____

    A. pylorus   B. peristalsis
    C. symbiosis   D. parthenogenesis

24. The corals belong to the phylum 24.____

    A. Mollusca   B. Porifera
    C. Arthropoda   D. Coelenterata

25. Three of the following substances are narcotics. The one that is NOT is 25.____

    A. chlorpromazine   B. nicotine
    C. morphine   D. cocaine

26. Hydrogen sulfide is USUALLY prepared in the laboratory by the action of 26.____

    A. hydrogen on hot sulfur
    B. hydrochloric acid on ferrous sulfide
    C. acid on sulfite
    D. sulfuric acid on copper

27. An unknown gas dissolves readily in water. The water solution turns red litmus blue. The gas reacts with hydrogen chloride gas, forming white fumes.
The unknown gas is PROBABLY 27.____

    A. nitric oxide   B. ammonia
    C. sulfur dioxide   D. hydrogen sulfide

28. Of the following, the one whose water solution will be basic in reaction is 0.1 molar 28.____

    A. HCl   B. $NaC_2H_3O_2$ C. NaCl   D. $HC_2H_3O_2$

29. An apple green flame test indicates the presence of 29.____

    A. chromium   B. sodium   C. strontium   D. barium

30. In the balanced chemical equation for the reaction between copper and dilute nitric acid, the coefficient before the nitric acid is 30.____

    A. 1   B. 3   C. 4   D. 8

31. The molecular weight of sodium hydroxide is 40.
To prepare 100 cc. of a 0.1 N solution would require a weight of sodium hydroxide, in grams, of 31.____

    A. 0.4   B. 2   C. 4   D. 400

32. Concentrated solutions of potassium hydroxide should be stored in bottles with stoppers made of 32.____

    A. glass   B. rubber   C. cork   D. aluminum

33. White phosphorus should be stored under 33.____

    A. carbon disulfide   B. carbon tetrachloride
    C. oil   D. water

34. It is dangerous to add concentrated sulfuric acid to 34.____

    A. calcium sulfate   B. sodium bisulfate
    C. potassium permanganate   D. clay

35. You should instruct students to carry concentrated sulfuric acid   35._____

   A. very carefully   B. in a covered metal can
   C. under no circumstances   D. in a cart

36. The formula for chloroform is   36._____

   A. CH_2Cl_2 B. $CHCl_3$ C. CH_3Cl D. $C_2H_4Cl_2$

37. *Wood* alcohol is the common name for   37._____

   A. ethyl alcohol   B. propyl alcohol
   C. glycerol   D. methyl alcohol

38. The FIRST thing to do if concentrated acid comes into contact with the skin is to   38._____

   A. wash with ammonia
   B. call a doctor
   C. pour sodium hydroxide over it
   D. wash with cold water for a long time

39. Hydrofluoric acid is GENERALLY stored in   39._____

   A. polyethylene bottles   B. glass bottles
   C. copper jars   D. platinum bottles

40. A liter is APPROXIMATELY equivalent to a(n)   40._____

   A. quart   B. pint   C. gallon   D. gill

41. The FIRST scientist to effect a nuclear reaction was   41._____

   A. Rutherford   B. J.J. Thomson
   C. Chadwick   D. Fermi

42. The chemical behavior of the atom is LARGELY determined by the   42._____

   A. atomic weight
   B. number of neutrons
   C. kind of charge in the nucleus
   D. electrons

43. Radioactive substances   43._____

   A. easily lose their orbital electrons
   B. have unstable nuclei
   C. gain electrons easily
   D. lack mesons

44. In the reaction $_7N^{15} + {}_1H^2 \rightarrow X + {}_1H^1$, X is   44._____

   A. $_9F^{17}$ B. $_8O^{15}$ C. $_8C^{14}$ D. $_7N^{16}$

45. In the reaction $C + O_2 \rightarrow CO_2$, the weight of CO_2, in grams, produced by burning 100 grams of carbon with 100 grams of oxygen is about (At. Wgts.: C = 12, O = 16)   45._____

   A. 100   B. 137   C. 150   D. 200

46. When sodium combines with chlorine, the sodium is

46.____

    A. oxidized and the chlorine is reduced
    B. reduced and the chlorine is oxidized
    C. oxidized and the chlorine remains unchanged
    D. unchanged while the chlorine is oxidized

47. An electric spark is passed through a mixture containing 3.2 grams of oxygen gas and 0.6 grams of hydrogen gas. After the explosion and subsequent cooling to room temperature, there are in the container

47.____

    A. 3.2 grams of water and 0.6 grams of hydrogen
    B. 3.6 grams of water and 0.2 grams of hydrogen
    C. 3.8 grams of water and 0 grams of hydrogen
    D. 0.9 grams of water and 2.9 grams of oxygen

48. The columns of the modern periodic table contain elements which resemble each other in

48.____

    A. the number of neutrons   B. valence
    C. density   D. appearance

49. Carbon forms a large number of compounds because

49.____

    A. of the ability of carbon atoms to form covalent linkages with each other
    B. of its small ionic radius
    C. it forms triple bonds
    D. it is very active

50. The SIMPLEST way to recover silver from a solution of one of its compounds is to

50.____

    A. distill the solution   B. use the thermit process
    C. add powdered zinc   D. decompose the solution

KEY (CORRECT ANSWERS)

1. D	11. B	21. C	31. A	41. A
2. C	12. A	22. B	32. B	42. D
3. B	13. C	23. B	33. D	43. B
4. C	14. B	24. D	34. C	44. D
5. A	15. D	25. A	35. C	45. B
6. B	16. A	26. B	36. B	46. A
7. D	17. A	27. B	37. D	47. B
8. D	18. C	28. B	38. D	48. B
9. C	19. A	29. D	39. A	49. A
10. D	20. A	30. D	40. A	50. C

TEST 3

DIRECTIONS: Each question or incomplete statement is followed by several suggested answers or completions. Select the one that BEST answers the question or completes the statement. *PRINT THE LETTER OF THE CORRECT ANSWER IN THE SPACE AT THE RIGHT.*

1. In a chemical reaction, the valence of the element arsenic was changed from +5 to 0.   1.____
    All of the following statements are true EXCEPT the one stating that arsenic

    A. oxidized something else   B. was reduced
    C. gained electrons   D. lost protons

2. The neutralization of a base by an acid ALWAYS produces   2.____

    A. soluble products   B. water
    C. gas   D. sodium chloride

3. The pH of an acid solution could be   3.____

    A. 5   B. 7   C. 9   D. 13

4. The CORRECT formula of the hydronium ion is   4.____

    A. OH^- B. H_3O^+ C. H_4O^+ D. $H+$

5. When $CaCO_3$ reacts with CHI, the products are   5.____

    A. CaO, H_2O and CO_2 B. $CaCl_2$, H_2O and CO_2
    C. $CaOCl$, H_2O and CO_2 D. $CaCl_2$, Cl_2, CO_2 and H_2O

6. A solution of a non-volatile solute in water   6.____

    A. boils at 100° C
    B. freezes below 0° C
    C. has a higher vapor pressure than water at the same temperature
    D. always has a volume equal to the combined volumes of solute and solvent

7. An unknown gas has a density of 1.5 grams per liter under standard conditions.   7.____
    Its molecular weight is about

    A. 33.6   B. 22.4   C. 11.2   D. 67.2

8. Of the following sequences, the one that CORRECTLY represents the non-metals in the   8.____
    order of their increasing activity as non-metals is

    A. F, Cl, Br, I   B. F, I, Cl, Br
    C. I, Cl, Br, F   D. I, Br, Cl, F

9. Carbon will NOT reduce the oxide of   9.____

    A. sodium   B. iron   C. zinc   D. copper

10. The valence of the metal in the compound $Ca_3(PO_4)_2$ is plus   10.____

    A. 1   B. 2   C. 3   D. 6

11. Covalent bonds are MOST commonly found in   11.____

    A. salts   B. bases
    C. inorganic solids   D. organic compounds

12. Al_2O_3 and CBr_4, are the correct formulae of the oxide of aluminum and the bromide of   12.____
carbon.
The formula of the compound aluminum carbide is

    A. AlC   B. Al_4C_3 C. Al_3C_4 D. Al_4C_2

13. A chalk and salt mixture could be separated into its components by   13.____

    A. subliming the salt out of the mixture
    B. adding water and distilling
    C. adding water, boiling, and filtering
    D. adding water, boiling, and cooling

14. The electrolysis of brine is used commercially to produce all of the following substances   14.____
EXCEPT

    A. sodium hydroxide   B. hydrogen
    C. chlorine   D. sodium chloride

15. In the Hall process, cryolite is used as a   15.____

    A. source of aluminum   B. solvent
    C. source of fluorine   D. solute

16. All of the following are present in pig iron as impurities EXCEPT   16.____

    A. silicon   B. phosphorus   C. molybdenum   D. sulfur

17. The compound MOST generally found in petroleum is   17.____

    A. $CHCl_3$ B. C_8H_{18} C. CH_5N D. $C_7H_{15}OH$

18. When a non-metallic oxide such as N_2O_5 is dissolved in water,   18.____

    A. the solution is acidic
    B. the solution is basic
    C. the solution may be either acidic or basic
    D. no chemical change occurs

19. In developing a photographic plate,   19.____

    A. sodium thiosulfate is used as a reducing agent
    B. it is left in the developer until all of the silver bromide has been developed
    C. no visible change takes place
    D. the exposed plate is reduced most rapidly where most light has been absorbed

20. The plastic lucite is a polymer of   20.____

    A. methyl methacrylate   B. styrene
    C. butadiene   D. acrylonitrile

21. MOST animal fats are classed as   21.____

    A. alcohols   B. esters   C. aldehydes   D. acids

22. Hydrogen should be prepared in the classroom by combining   22.____

    A. sodium and hydrochloric acid
    B. zinc and sulfuric acid
    C. potassium chlorate and hydrochloric acid
    D. iron oxide and steam

23. The formula for baking soda is   23.____

    A. Na_2CO_3 B. $NaOH$ C. $NaHCO_3$ D. Na_2SO_4

24. The chemist GENERALLY credited with discovering deuterium is   24.____

    A. Hall   B. Urey
    C. Fermi   D. Oppenheimer

25. Thermit mixture is composed of   25.____

    A. magnesium and iron oxide
    B. iron and aluminum oxide
    C. aluminum and iron oxide
    D. magnesium and barium peroxide

26. The statement, *It is easier to raise a load with pulleys,* means that for the given load,   26.____
there is a reduction in the required

    A. force   B. work   C. distance   D. power

27. If, when three forces are applied to a body, the body is at rest, the resultant of these   27.____
forces is

    A. the weight of the object
    B. more than the largest force
    C. zero
    D. the equilibrant of the object

28. Reducing friction has no effect on the   28.____

    A. actual mechanical advantage
    B. efficiency
    C. ideal mechanical advantage
    D. work input

29. Machines can multiply   29.____

    A. work   B. energy   C. force   D. efficiency

30. Weights of 3 lb. and 7 lb. hang from a bar which is supported by a spring scale.   30.____
Neglecting the weight of the bar, the weight, in pounds, registered by the scale is

    A. 2.5   B. 4   C. 10   D. 21

31. A body starts from rest and falls freely for four seconds. The distance, in feet, the body will fall (neglecting air resistance) is   31.____

    A. 64   B. 96   C. 256   D. 512

32. The width of the film, in inches, used in a 35 mm camera is   32.____

    A. 1   B. 1.4   C. 2.5   D. 3.5

33. The pressure cooker cooks food more rapidly because the   33.____

    A. water boils more rapidly
    B. water boils at a higher temperature
    C. less water is used
    D. pressure is reduced below normal

34. Any two objects of equal weight are necessarily at the same temperature if   34.____

    A. they contain equal amounts of heat
    B. they lose heat at equal rates
    C. neither loses heat to the other when they are in contact
    D. their molecules have equal average speeds

35. Heat may be measured by   35.____

    A. temperature change in a known quantity of water
    B. the expansion of mercury
    C. the bending of a bimetallic strip
    D. the expansion of hydrogen

36. The quantity of heat, in calories, required to change 10 grams of ice at 0° C to water at 20° C is   36.____

    A. 100   B. 200   C. 1000   D. 5600

37. To double the pressure in a fixed volume of a gas at 0° C, its temperature, in $^\circ$ C, must be raised to   37.____

    A. 100   B. 273   C. 373   D. 546

38. An object is placed 8 inches from a convex lens of 4 inch focal length. The image formed will be   38.____

    A. larger than the object
    B. smaller than the object
    C. the same size as the object
    D. virtual

39. When light strikes the prisms in binoculars, it will be   39.____

    A. reflected   B. refracted
    C. dispersed   D. absorbed

40. Evidence that light is a transverse wave phenomenon is obtained from   40.____

    A. beats   B. polarization
    C. photoelectric effect   D. interference

41. The failure of a lens to focus, at a point, light of different colors is called 41.____

    A. interference   B. spherical aberration
    C. polarization   D. chromatic aberration

42. Two sounds of the same wavelength MUST have the same 42.____

    A. amplitude   B. frequency   C. intensity   D. quality

43. The human ear cannot distinguish tones that differ in 43.____

    A. phase   B. quality   C. intensity   D. pitch

44. Of the following, the one that is at MAXIMUM when resonance occurs in an electrical circuit is 44.____

    A. impedance   B. resistance   C. reactance   D. current

45. Electromagnetic waves radiated into space are called _____ waves. 45.____

    A. rectified   B. carrier
    C. stationary   D. polarized

46. A TV broadcasting station transmits the picture (video signal) by means of _____ modulation of _____ frequency waves. 46.____

    A. frequency; high   B. amplitude; high
    C. frequency; low   D. amplitude; low

47. The emission of electrons from certain metals when they are exposed to light is known as the _____ effect. 47.____

    A. thermionic   B. Edison
    C. photoelectric   D. thermoelectric

48. The process of varying the amplitude of a carrier wave is called 48.____

    A. modulation   B. regeneration
    C. oscillation   D. rectification

49. A transformer may be used to increase 49.____

    A. energy   B. power   C. voltage   D. wattage

50. An induction coil 50.____

    A. produces a large current
    B. changes AC to DC
    C. produces a high voltage
    D. steps down high voltages

KEY (CORRECT ANSWERS)

1.	D	11.	D	21.	B	31.	C	41.	D
2.	B	12.	B	22.	B	32.	B	42.	B
3.	A	13.	C	23.	C	33.	B	43.	A
4.	B	14.	D	24.	B	34.	C	44.	C
5.	B	15.	B	25.	C	35.	A	45.	B
6.	B	16.	C	26.	A	36.	C	46.	B
7.	A	17.	B	27.	C	37.	B	47.	C
8.	D	18.	A	28.	C	38.	C	48.	A
9.	A	19.	D	29.	C	39.	A	49.	C
10.	B	20.	A	30.	C	40.	B	50.	C

TEST 4

DIRECTIONS: Each question or incomplete statement is followed by several suggested answers or completions. Select the one that BEST answers the question or completes the statement. *PRINT THE LETTER OF THE CORRECT ANSWER IN THE SPACE AT THE RIGHT.*

1. The part NOT found in an AC generator is a(n)   1.____

    A. field magnet   B. armature
    C. brush(es)   D. commutator

2. To protect a delicate watch from a magnetic field, its case should be made of   2.____

    A. cobalt   B. aluminum
    C. soft iron   D. steel

3. The electrical device MOST similar to a galvanometer in operation is the   3.____

    A. bell   B. electromagnet
    C. motor   D. fuse

4. A hand generator is easier to turn when the external circuit is open.   4.____
This is BEST explained by a principle stated by

    A. Oersted   B. Ampere   C. Ohm   D. Lenz

5. *60 cycle* current refers to   5.____

    A. wavelength   B. amplitude
    C. frequency   D. velocity

6. One end of a metal rod is brought near the north pole of a magnet, and it is noted that   6.____
they attract.
This indicates that the metal rod is

    A. a permanent magnet   B. not a magnet
    C. a magnetic substance   D. made of iron

7. One coulomb per second defines one   7.____

    A. volt   B. watt   C. ampere   D. ohm

8. Electricity is stored in a   8.____

    A. dry cell   B. condenser
    C. storage battery   D. generator

9. Increasing the distance between the plates of a charged capacitor   9.____

    A. *increases* the potential difference
    B. *decreases* the potential difference
    C. *decreases* the amount of charge
    D. *increases* the amount of charge

10. A radioactive emission not bent by a magnetic field is a(n)   10.____

    A. proton   B. gamma ray
    C. beta particle   D. alpha particle

11. $_4Be^9$ means that the number of protons in a beryllium nucleus is   11.____

    A.   4   B.   5   C.   9   D.   13

12. *Isotopes* is the name given to elements that have   12.____

    A.   the same atomic number but different atomic mass
    B.   the same atomic mass but different atomic number
    C.   the same atomic mass and the same atomic number but different chemical properties
    D.   similar chemical properties although they differ in both atomic mass and atomic number

13. Ionization is the basis for the   13.____

    A.   Geiger counter and scintillation counter
    B.   Geiger counter and cloud chamber
    C.   cloud chamber and scintillation counter
    D.   Geiger counter, cloud chamber, and scintillation counter

14. Atomic mass is determined by   14.____

    A.   protons   B.   neutrons
    C.   protons plus neutrons   D.   protons minus neutrons

15. The mass of a nucleus, as compared with the sum of the masses of the particles which compose it, is   15.____

    A.   slightly greater   B.   much greater
    C.   equal   D.   slightly less

16. To an observer on Earth, the BRIGHTEST planet is   16.____

    A.   Jupiter   B.   Saturn   C.   Mars   D.   Venus

17. The Russian Lunik revolves around the   17.____

    A.   sun outside the earth's orbit
    B.   sun inside the earth's orbit
    C.   moon
    D.   earth

18. The Northern Cross lies in the constellation   18.____

    A.   Cygnus   B.   Bootes   C.   Lyra   D.   Pegasus

19. A galaxy visible to the unaided eye lies in the constellation   19.____

    A.   Andromeda   B.   Ursa Minor
    C.   Auriga   D.   Canis Major

20. A rock composed of angular fragments cemented together into a coherent mass is a   20.____

    A.   breccia   B.   tufa   C.   conglomerate   D.   dacite

21. In Moh's scale of mineral hardness, quartz is number   21.____

    A.   5   B.   6   C.   7   D.   8

22. A rock which shows foliated structure is   22.____

   A. marble   B. serpentine   C. schist   D. quartzite

23. A river is classified as mature when it includes a   23.____

   A. chain of lakes in its course
   B. gorge
   C. series of meanders
   D. series of rapids

24. On a Mercator projection, a straight line joining New York City and Liverpool   24.____

   A. has constant direction
   B. has constant scale
   C. is the arc of a great circle
   D. has a larger scale near Liverpool than near New York

25. An esker is a   25.____

   A. winding, roughly stratified glacial ridge
   B. linear, unstratified glacial ridge
   C. roughly circular glacial mound
   D. series of glacial elevations and depressions

26. An example of an active volcano of the *quiet* type is   26.____

   A. Krakatoa   B. Mauna Loa
   C. Mt. Lassen   D. Mt. Vesuvius

27. Stone Mt., Georgia is classified as a   27.____

   A. butte   B. mesa
   C. monadnock   D. volcanic neck

28. The velocity of escape of a projectile from the Earth, in number of miles per hour, is   28.____
    about

   A. 7,000   B. 18,000   C. 25,000   D. 35,000

29. An outstanding example of a glacial trough is the   29.____

   A. Grand Canyon of the Colorado
   B. Yellowstone Canyon in Yellowstone National Park
   C. Yosemite Valley in Yosemite National Park
   D. Zion Canyon in Zion National Park

30. The Keewatin Glacier of the Pleistocene ice age was centered in   30.____

   A. north central Canada   B. Labrador
   C. Alaska   D. Greenland

31. Lost rivers or underground streams are MOST likely to occur in regions whose bedrock is   31.____

   A. limestone   B. slate
   C. granite   D. conglomerate

32. The Royal Gorge of the Arkansas River represents a river valley which is   32.____

    A. young   B. mature   C. old   D. subdued

33. Sink holes are the result of the work of   33.____

    A. earthquakes   B. underground water
    C. streams   D. glaciers

34. The mineral which is LEAST susceptible to chemical weathering is   34.____

    A. feldspar   B. hornblends
    C. augite   D. quartz

35. Of the following, the mountains of GREATEST geologic age are the   35.____

    A. Appalachians   B. Rockies
    C. Sierra Nevadas   D. Cascades

36. Laccoliths are found in   36.____

    A. domed mountains   B. block mountains
    C. folded mountains   D. volcanoes

37. The normal percentage of dissolved mineral matter in sea water (by weight) is APPROX-   37.____
    IMATELY

    A. 1.5   B. 2.5   C. 3.5   D. 4.5

38. A shoreline formed as a result of submergence is a _____ shoreline.   38.____

    A. coastal plain   B. delta
    C. fiord   D. volcano

39. Spring tides occur at   39.____

    A. full moon *only*
    B. new moon *only*
    C. both full and new moon
    D. first and last quarter phases

40. An annular eclipse of the sun takes place at the phase of the moon called   40.____

    A. new moon   B. new gibbous
    C. new crescent   D. full moon

41. When it is noon, Eastern Standard Time, in New York City, the standard time at the 120W   41.____
    meridian is

    A. 9 A.M.   B. 10 A.M.   C. 2 P.M.   D. 3 P.M.

42. On June 21, in New York City, the sun   42.____

    A. rises in the northeast
    B. sets in the southwest
    C. reaches the zenith at local noon
    D. is north of the zenith at local noon

43. The Palisades of New Jersey originated as an igneous intrusion during the period known   43.____
    as

    A. Eocene   B. Cretaceous
    C. Permian   D. Triassic

44. A region whose warmest monthly temperature average is 80° F, while its coldest monthly   44.____
    temperature average is 77° F, MUST have a climate typified as

    A. marine west coast   B. Mediterranean
    C. tropical desert   D. tropical rainforest

45. A necessary condition for the formation of sleet is a   45.____

    A. cold front   B. strong pressure gradient
    C. steep lapse rate   D. temperature inversion

46. The dry adiabetic lapse rate per 1000 feet is   46.____

    A. 2.5° F   B. 3.5° F   C. 4.5° F   D. 5.5° F

47. The prevailing wind at 40S latitude is   47.____

    A. northwesterly   B. northeasterly
    C. southwesterly   D. southeasterly

48. The European equivalent of the American Chinook wind is known as the   48.____

    A. bora   B. buran   C. foehn   D. mistral

49. Cumulonimbus clouds are MOST likely to occur in connection with a(n) _____ air mass.   49.____

    A. mTk   B. mTw   C. cPk   D. cPw

50. At perigee, our moon's distance, expressed in miles, from the earth is about   50.____

    A. 205,000   B. 220,000   C. 235,000   D. 245,000

KEY (CORRECT ANSWERS)

1. D	11. A	21. C	31. A	41. A
2. C	12. A	22. C	32. A	42. A
3. C	13. B	23. D	33. B	43. D
4. D	14. C	24. A	34. D	44. D
5. C	15. D	25. A	35. A	45. D
6. C	16. D	26. B	36. A	46. D
7. C	17. A	27. C	37. C	47. A
8. B	18. A	28. C	38. C	48. C
9. A	19. A	29. C	39. C	49. A
10. B	20. A	30. A	40. A	50. B

EXAMINATION SECTION
TEST 1

DIRECTIONS: Each question or incomplete statement is followed by several suggested answers or completions. Select the one that BEST answers the question or completes the statement. *PRINT THE LETTER OF THE CORRECT ANSWER IN THE SPACE AT THE RIGHT.*

1. $\sqrt{465}$ is MOST NEARLY   1.____

    A.   20.56   B.   21.13   C.   21.34   D.   21.56

2. $90°$ is MOST NEARLY equal to _____ radians.   2.____

    A.   0.5   B.   1.5   C.   2.5   D.   3.5

3. When .68 feet is converted to inches, the result is MOST NEARLY   3.____

    A.   7 7/8"   B.   8"   C.   8 1/8"   D.   8 1/4"

4. A 100' guy wire, stretched tight from the top of a vertical pole, makes a $60°$ angle with the   4.____
    level ground.
    The height of this pole, in feet, is MOST NEARLY (sin $60°$ = .867, cos $60°$ = .500)

    A.   50   B.   87   C.   100   D.   200

5. The area of a $120°$ sector of a circle whose radius is 3" is MOST NEARLY _____   5.____
    square inches.

    A.   7.9   B.   9.42   C.   11.3   D.   12.5

6. The product $\dfrac{6xy}{x^2-4} \cdot \dfrac{5x-10}{3xy}$ is equal to   6.____

    A. $\dfrac{2xy}{x^2-40}$ B. $\dfrac{30x^2}{x^2y}$ C. $\dfrac{10}{x+2}$ D. $\dfrac{18x^3y}{x+10}$

7. The $\sin^2 x$ is equal to   7.____

    A. $1-2\cos^2 x$ B. $1+2\cos^2 x$
    C. $1+\cos^2 x$ D. $1-\cos^2 x$

8. The volume of a cylinder with a radius of r and height h is   8.____

    A. $\pi r^2 h$ B. $2\pi rh$ C. $2\pi r^2 h$ D. $4\pi r^2 h$

9. The expression $\sqrt{28} - \sqrt{7}$ reduces to   9.____

    A. $\sqrt{7}$ B. $3\sqrt{7}$ C. $\sqrt{21}$ D. $-\sqrt{35}$

10. If sin 2x = 1, then x is   10.____

    A. 30°   B. 45°   C. 60°   D. 75°

11. The expression $\dfrac{x^{-2}y^2}{y} - \dfrac{x^2}{x^4} + y^0$ reduces to   11.____

    A. $\dfrac{xy}{x^4}$ B. $\dfrac{y^2}{y - x^4}$ C. $\dfrac{y-1}{x^2+1}$ D. $\dfrac{y-1}{x^2+y}$

12. If the coordinates of E and F in the X-Y plane are (1,-1) and (4,3), respectively, then the length of line E-F is   12.____

    A. 4   B. 5   C. 6   D. 7

13. The sum of the interior angles of a regular octagon is   13.____

    A. 360°   B. 540°   C. 1080°   D. 1800°

14. The number of cubic yards of concrete required to fill eighteen 24" diameter steel pipe piles 150 feet long is MOST NEARLY   14.____

    A. 80   B. 155   C. 315   D. 630

15. A flow of 100 gallons per second for a day is, in millions of gallons per day, MOST NEARLY equal to   15.____

    A. 7.93   B. 8.05   C. 8.64   D. 9.20

16. It takes 4 hours for a certain pump to drain an excavation by itself. It takes a second pump 6 hours to drain that same excavation working by itself.
If both pumps are used together, the length of time it will take to drain the excavation is MOST NEARLY _____ minutes.   16.____

    A. 120   B. 144   C. 300   D. 600

17. The area, in square yards, of a trapezoid which has an altitude of 81 feet perpendicular to two parallel sides which are 125 feet and 275 feet long, respectively, is MOST NEARLY   17.____

    A. 600   B. 1,800   C. 5,400   D. 10,400

18. The expression $\dfrac{7!}{180}$ reduces to   18.____

    A. 28   B. 56   C. 112   D. 224

19. If Log 2 = .3010 and Log 3 = .4771, then Log 324 is MOST NEARLY   19.____

    A. 1.9898   B. 2.2094   C. 2.5104   D. 2.6387

20. An isosceles right triangle has a(n) _____ angle.   20.____

    A. obtuse   B. 45°   C. 60°   D. 30°

21. The number of cubic yards of topsoil required to cover a rectangular tract of land 108 feet 21.____
long by 96 feet wide to a depth of 6 inches is MOST NEARLY

    A. 192   B. 198   C. 215   D. 230

22. If the payment for steel is 25 cents per pound and a 1-inch-square bar 1 foot long weighs 22.____
3.4#, then the payment for a steel bar 2" x 4" in cross section 8' long is

    A. $8.10   B. $32.80   C. $16.40   D. $54.40

23. Expressed in degrees, 57° - 35' - 20" is MOST NEARLY   23.____

    A. 57.585   B. 57.587   C. 57.589   D. 57.591

24.   24.____

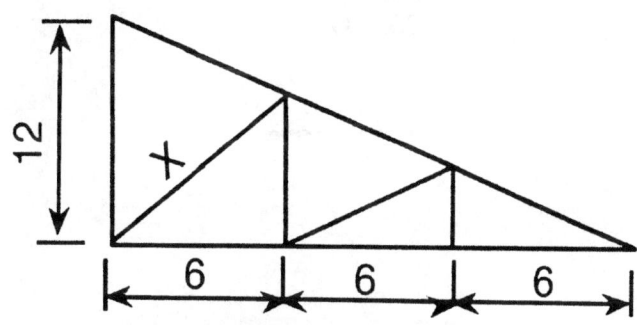

In the sketch shown above, the length of x is

    A. 8.0   B. 9.0   C. 9.5   D. 10.0

25. In Circle "O," inscribed angle ABC and central angle AOC have the same intercepted arc 25.____
AC in common. Of the following relationships between angle AOC and angle ABC, the
one which is TRUE is that

    A. angle ABC equals angle AOC
    B. angle AOC equals one-half angle ABC
    C. angle ABC equals one-half angle AOC
    D. nothing can be said about their relative sizes solely on the basis of the information
       given

KEY (CORRECT ANSWERS)

1.	D	11.	C
2.	B	12.	B
3.	C	13.	C
4.	B	14.	C
5.	B	15.	C
6.	C	16.	B
7.	D	17.	B
8.	A	18.	A
9.	A	19.	C
10.	B	20.	B

21.	A
22.	D
23.	C
24.	D
25.	C

———

TEST 2

DIRECTIONS: Each question or incomplete statement is followed by several suggested answers or completions. Select the one that BEST answers the question or completes the statement. *PRINT THE LETTER OF THE CORRECT ANSWER IN THE SPACE AT THE RIGHT.*

1. In pounds per square inch above absolute 0, atmospheric pressure at sea level is MOST NEARLY

   A. 4.7   B. 14.7   C. 19.92   D. 29.92

   1.____

2. Of the following, the one that is a unit in which kinetic energy is expressed is

   A. feet
   B. foot pounds
   C. foot pounds/second
   D. foot pounds per second squared

   2.____

3. The formula for methane gas is

   A. CH_2 B. CH_4 C. C_2H_2 D. C_2H_4

   3.____

4. The substance represented by the formula PbS is known as

   A. galena   B. caustic soda
   C. zinc blende   D. litharge

   4.____

5. Of the following statements about water, the one which is TRUE is that

   A. it is practically incompressible
   B. it is most dense at 32° F
   C. a unit volume of water weighs less than the same volume of alcohol
   D. it has no surface tension

   5.____

6. A 50-ohm resistor and a 100-ohm resistor are connected in series to a 120-volt source. Heat will be developed

   A. in the 50-ohm resistor at a greater rate
   B. in the 100-ohm resistor at a greater rate
   C. in both resistors at the same rate
   D. at a greater rate in whichever resistor is connected to the positive side of the voltage source

   6.____

7. An object falling freely from rest for one-half second will drop a distance of MOST NEARLY _____ feet.

   A. 4   B. 8   C. 16   D. 32

   7.____

8. The horsepower required to lift a 2,200-pound weight a vertical distance of 3 feet in one-half second is MOST NEARLY (HP = $\frac{wh}{550}$)

   A. 3   B. 12   C. 24   D. 30

   8.____

9. When 2 amps flow through a 20-ohm resistor, the power dissipated by this resistor is MOST NEARLY _____ watts.

    A. 10   B. 20   C. 40   D. 80

9.____

10. When the velocity of an object following a circular path is doubled, the centripetal force necessary to keep it in its circular path is

    A. halved   B. unchanged
    C. doubled   D. quadrupled

10.____

11. The potential difference across a 3-ohm resistor is 12 volts.
The current flowing through this resistor is MOST NEARLY _____ amps.

    A. 2   B. 4   C. 6   D. 27

11.____

12. The equivalent on the Fahrenheit scale of 100 degrees Centigrade is

    A. 100° B. 132° C. 180° D. 212°

12.____

13. Of the following, the chemical that is an organic compound is

    A. C_6H_6 B. HNO_3 C. H_2SO_3 D. SiO_2

13.____

14. A substance which changes the speed of a chemical reaction without itself being permanently changed is known as

    A. amorphous   B. an amphoteric compound
    C. a catalyst   D. a salt

14.____

15. A chemical reaction accompanied by the evolution of heat is known as

    A. an endothermic reaction   B. an exothermic reaction
    C. neutralization   D. nuclear fission

15.____

16. The mixing of gases, liquids, and solids by means of molecular motion is called

    A. diffusion   B. effervescence
    C. decomposition   D. filtration

16.____

17. The ideal mechanical advantage of the pulley system pictured at the right is MOST NEARLY
    A. 2
    B. 3
    C. 4
    D. 5

17.____

18. Of the following colors of light, the one with the LONGEST wavelength is

    A. red   B. orange   C. yellow   D. blue

18.____

19.   19._____

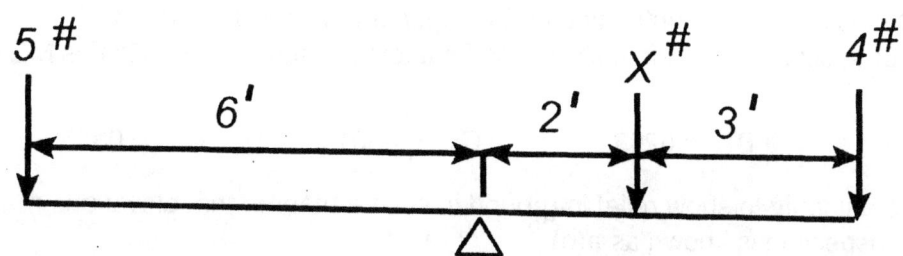

In the lever shown in the sketch above, the magnitude of force X needed to balance the lever is MOST NEARLY _____ 1bs.

   A. 3.0   B. 4.5   C. 5.0   D. 6.0

20. A 2-candlepower lamp is placed 2 ft. from a photometer screen. Another lamp placed 6 feet from the screen produces equal illumination on the screen.   20._____
The illumination of the second lamp is MOST NEARLY _____ cp.

   A. 15   B. 18   C. 20   D. 25

21. If, in the diagram shown at the right, the bearing of line OY is S65° E, then the bearing of line OX is   21._____

   A. S17° E
   B. N17° E
   C. N17° W
   D. S17° W

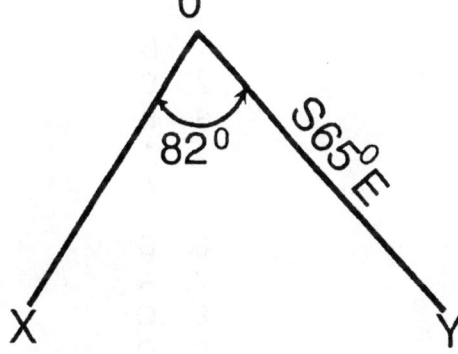

22. If a backsight on a benchmark whose elevation is 116.75' is 8.42' and the foresight on a turning point is 9.35', then the elevation of the turning point is   22._____

   A. 119.71'   B. 118.53'   C. 117.68'   D. 115.82'

23.   23._____

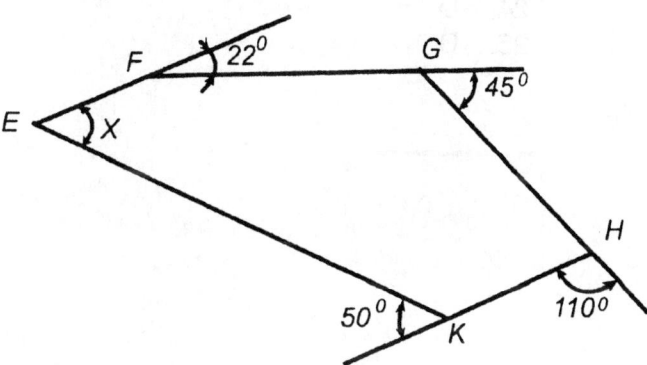

In the closed traverse shown above, the angle X is

   A. 33°   B. 40°   C. 47°   D. 55°

24. If a 100-foot-long steel tape contracts 0.00645' upon a temperature drop of 10°
F, then the contraction of an 85-foot steel tape for a temperature drop of 65° F is MOST
NEARLY

    A. 0.0223'   B. 0.0268'   C. 0.0301'   D. 0.0355'

24._____

25. A map made primarily to show relief in ground in such a manner that elevations may be
obtained by inspection is known as a(n) _____ map.

    A. planimetric   B. isogonic
    C. railroad   D. topographic

25._____

KEY (CORRECT ANSWERS)

1.	B		11.	B
2.	B		12.	D
3.	B		13.	A
4.	A		14.	C
5.	A		15.	B
6.	B		16.	A
7.	A		17.	A
8.	C		18	A
9.	D		19.	C
10.	D		20.	B

21.	D
22.	D
23.	C
24.	D
25.	D

ARITHMETICAL REASONING

EXAMINATION SECTION
TEST 1

DIRECTIONS: Each question or incomplete statement is followed by several suggested answers or completions. Select the one that BEST answers the question or completes the statement. *PRINT THE LETTER OF THE CORRECT ANSWER IN THE SPACE AT THE RIGHT.*

1. A canvas tarpaulin measures 6 feet by 9 feet.
   The LARGEST circular area that can be covered completely by this tarpaulin is a circle with a diameter of _____ feet.

   A. 9   B. 8   C. 7   D. 6

   1.____

2. The population of Maple Grove was 1,000 in 2006. In 2007, the population increased 40 percent, but in 2008, 2009, and 2010, the population decreased 20 percent, 10 percent, and 25 percent, respectively. (For each year, the percentage change in population is based upon a comparison with the preceding year.)
   At the end of this period, the population was MOST NEARLY

   A. 900   B. 850   C. 800   D. 750

   2.____

3. The ratio of boys to girls in one school is 6 to 4. A second school contains half as many boys and twice as many girls as the first.
   The one of the following statements that is MOST accurate is that

   A. both schools have the same number of pupils
   B. the first school has 10 percent more pupils than the second
   C. the second school has 10 percent more pupils than the first
   D. there is not sufficient information to reach any conclusion about which school has more pupils

   3.____

4. In a certain city, X number of cases of malaria have occurred over a 10-year period, resulting in Y number of deaths.
   The AVERAGE annual death rate from malaria in this city is

   A. Y/10   B. 10/X   C. 10-X/Y   D. $\dfrac{Y(10X)}{X+Y}$

   4.____

5. A firemen's softball team wins 6 games out of the first 9 played. They go on to win all their remaining games and finish the season with a final average of games won of .750.
   The TOTAL number of games they played that season was

   A. 10   B. 12   C. 15   D. 18

   5.____

6. While inspecting a cylindrical gravity tank for an automatic sprinkler system, a chief observes that the water in the tank is 10 feet deep and that the tank has a diameter of 9 feet. He asks the building manager how many gallons are in the tank and receives the reply, *About 10,000.* (Cubic foot of water contains 7 1/2 gallons.) Based on his own observation and calculations, the chief should

   6.____

A. agree that the manager's answer is probably correct
B. disagree with the manager's answer; the answer is more nearly 20,000 gallons
C. disagree with the manager's answer; the answer is more nearly 15,000 gallons
D. disagree with the manager's answer; the answer is more nearly 5,000 gallons

7. The diagram at the right represents the storage space of a fire engine. The amount of space available for the storage of hose in the fire engine is MOST NEARLY _____ cubic feet.

7.____

A. 40
B. 75
C. 540
D. 600

8. If a piece of rope 100 feet long is cut so that one piece is 2/3 as long as the other piece, the length of the longer piece must be _____ feet.

8.____

A. 60   B. 66 2/3   C. 70   D. 75

9. A water tank has a discharge valve which is capable of emptying the tank when full in two hours. It also has an inlet valve which can fill the tank, when empty, in four hours and a second inlet valve which can fill the tank, when empty, in six hours.
If the tank is full and all three valves are opened fully, with water flowing through each valve to capacity, the tank will be emptied in _____ hours.

9.____

A. 2
B. 6
C. 12
D. a period of time which cannot be determined from the information given

10. Final grades in a history course are determined as follows:
    Class recitations - weight 50
    Weekly quizzes - weight 25
    Final examination - weight 25
A student has an average of 60 on a class recitation and 80 on weekly quizzes.
In order to receive a final grade of 75, he must obtain on his final examination a grade of

10 ____

A. 75   B. 80   C. 90   D. 100

11. Suppose that 8 inches of snow contribute as much water to the reservoir system as one inch of rain.
If, during a snowstorm, an average of 12 inches of snow fell during a six-hour period, with drifts as high as three feet, the addition to the water supply as a result of this snowfall ultimately will be the equivalent of _____ inches of rain.

11.____

A. 1 1/2
B. 3
C. 4 1/2
D. an amount of rain which cannot be determined from the information given

120

12. A fire engine carries 900 feet of 2 1/2" hose, 500 feet of 2" hose, and 350 feet of 1 1/2"   12.____
    hose.
    Of the total hose carried, the percentage of 1 1/2" hose is MOST NEARLY

    A. 35   B. 30   C. 25   D. 20

13. An engine company made 96 runs in the month of April, which was a decrease of 20%   13.____
    from the number of runs made in March.
    The number of runs made in March was MOST NEARLY

    A. 136   B. 128   C. 120   D. 110

14. A water tank has a capacity of 6,000 gallons. Connected to the tank is a pump capable of   14.____
    supplying water at the rate of 25 gallons per minute, which goes into operation automati-
    cally when the water in the tank falls to the one-half mark.
    If we start with a full tank and drain the water from the tank at the rate of 50 gallons a
    minute, the tank can continue supplying water at the required rate for_____ hours.

    A. 2 1/2   B. 3   C. 3 1/2   D. 4

15. Three firemen are assigned the task of cleaning fire apparatus which usually takes three   15.____
    men five hours to complete. After they have been working three hours, three additional
    firemen are assigned to help them. Assuming that they all work at the normal rate, the
    assignment of the additional men will reduce the time required to complete the task by
    _____ minutes.

    A. 20   B. 30   C. 50   D. 60

16. Assume that at the beginning of the calendar year, an employee was earning $48,000   16.____
    per year. On July 1st, he received an increase of $2,400 per year. On November 1st, he
    was promoted to a position paying $60,000 per year. The total earnings for the year were
    MOST NEARLY

    A. $51,000   B. $49,000   C. $50,000   D. $53,000

17. Engine A leaves its firehouse at 1:48 P.M. and travels 3 miles to a fire at an average   17.____
    speed of 30 miles per hour. Engine B leaves its firehouse at 1:51 P.M. and travels 6 miles
    to the same fire at an average speed of 40 miles per hour.
    From the above facts, we may conclude that Engine A arrives _____ minutes _____
    Engine B.

    A. 3; before   B. 6; before
    C. 3; after   D. 6; after

18. A widely used formula for calculating the quantity of water discharged from a hose is   18.____
    $GPM = 29.7d^2/P$, where GPM = gallons per minute, d = diameter of the nozzle in inches,
    and P = pressure at the nozzle in pounds per square inch.
    If it takes 1 minute to extinguish a fire using a 1 1/2" nozzle at 100 pounds pressure per
    square inch, the number of gallons discharged is, according to the above formula,
    MOST NEARLY

    A. 730   B. 650   C. 690   D. 670

121

19. The spring of a spring balance will stretch in proportion to the amount of weight placed   19.____
    on the balance.
    If a 2-pound weight placed on a certain balance stretches the spring 1/4", then a
    stretch in the spring of 1 3/4" will be caused by a weight of _____ lbs.

    A. 10   B. 12   C. 14   D. 16

20. In a yard 100 feet by 60 feet, a dog is tied by a leash to a stake driven into the ground in   20.____
    the center of the yard.
    If the dog is to be kept from going off the property, the MAXIMUM acceptable length of
    the leash is _____ feet.

    A. 60   B. 50   C. 30   D. 28

21. From a length of pipe 10 feet long, a 3 1/3 foot piece is to be cut.   21.____
    If the diameter of the 10-foot length is 5 inches, the diameter of the piece to be cut will
    be

    A. 5"   B. 2 1/3"   C. 2"   D. 1 2/3"

22. A certain crew consists of one foreman who is paid $15.00 per hour, 2 carpenters who   22.____
    are paid $12.60 per hour, 4 helpers who are paid $10.50 per hour, and 10 laborers who
    are paid $7.50 per hour.
    The average hourly earnings of the members of the crew is MOST NEARLY

    A. $11.40   B. $10.50   C. $10.05   D. $9.30

23. The fraction which is equivalent to the sum of .125, .25, .375, and .0625 is   23.____

    A. 5/8   B. 13/16   C. 7/8   D. 15/16

24. If the pay period of an employee is changed from every two weeks to twice a month, his   24.____
    gross pay (before deductions) from each pay period will

    A. increase by one-tenth
    B. increase by one-twelfth
    C. decrease by one-thirteenth
    D. decrease by one-fifteenth

25. In a certain state, the automobile license tags consist of two letters followed by three dig-   25.____
    its, e.g., AA-122. The MAXIMUM number of different combinations of numbers and let-
    ters which can be obtained under this system is MOST NEARLY

    A. 13,500   B. 75,000   C. 325,000   D. 675,000

————

KEY (CORRECT ANSWERS)

1.	D	11.	A
2.	D	12.	D
3.	C	13.	C
4.	A	14.	B
5.	B	15.	D
6.	D	16.	A
7.	C	17.	B
8.	A	18.	D
9.	C	19.	C
10.	D	20.	C

21.	A
22.	D
23.	B
24.	B
25.	D

SOLUTIONS TO PROBLEMS

1. The largest circular area completely covered by the tarpaulin would have a diameter of the lesser of 6 ft. and 9 ft.

2. At the end of 2010, the population was $(1000)(1.40)(.80)(.90)(.75) = 756 \approx 750$.

3. Let 6x and 4x represent the number of boys and girls, respectively, at the first school. Then, 3x and 8x will represent the number of boys and girls, respectively, at the second school. The enrollment of the second school, 11x, is 10% higher than the enrollment at the first school, 10x.

4. Since Y deaths have occurred over a 10-year period due to malaria, the annual death rate caused by malaria is Y/10. X, the number of cases of malaria, has no effect on the annual death rate.

5. Let x = number of games played, after the first 9 games. Then, $(6+x)/(9+x) = .750$. Solving, x = 3. The total number of games played = 9 + 3 = 12.

6. Volume = $(\pi) (4.5)^2 (10) \approx 636$ cu.ft. Then, $(636)(7\ 1/2) = 4770 \approx 5000$

7. 15x8x3 = 360; 15x6x2 = 180; 360 + 180 = 540 cu.ft.

8. Let 2x and 3x represent the two pieces. Then, 2x + 3x = 100. Solving, x = 20. The longer piece = (3)(20) = 60 ft.

9. Let x = number of hours required. Then, $\frac{x}{2} - \frac{x}{4} - \frac{x}{6} = 1$ Simplifying, x/12 = 1. Thus, x = 12

10. Let x = final exam grade. Then, $(60)(.50) + (80)(.25) + (x)(.25) = 75$. Simplifying, 50 + ,25x = 75. Solving, x = 100

11. If 8 in. of snow contribute 1 in. of rain, then 12 in. of snow contribute (1)(12/8) = 1 1/2 in. of rain.

12. $350 \div (900+500+350) = .20 = 20\%$

13. The number of runs in March was $96 \div .80 = 120$

14. The time required to extract 3000 gallons at 50 gallons per minute = $3000 \div 50 = 60$ min. = 1 hour. At this point, the tank is half full. Also, a pump begins replenishing the tank at 25 gallons per minute. Thus, the effect on draining has been slowed to 50 - 25 = 25 gallons per minute. To drain the remaining 3000 gallons will require $3000 \div 25 = 120$ minutes = 2 hours. Total draining time = 3 hours.

15. (3)(5) = 15 man-hours. After 3 hours, 9 man-hours have been used. At this point, 6 men are working, and since only 6 man-hours remaining, the time needed is 1 hour = 60 minutes.

16. ($48,000)(1/2) + ($50,400)(1/3) + ($60,000)(1/6) = $50,800 ≈ $51,000

17. Engine A requires (3)(60/30) = 6 minutes to get to the fire.
So, Engine A arrives at 1:54 PM. Engine B requires (6)(60/40) = 9 minutes to get to the fire. So, Engine B arrives at 2:00 PM. Thus, Engine A arrives 6 minutes before Engine B.

18. GPM = $(29.7)(1.5)^2(\sqrt{100})$ = 668.25 ≈ 670

19. Let x = required number of pounds. Then, 2/x = 1/4/1 3/4.
So, 1/4x = 3 1/2. Solving, x = 14

20. The shorter of the two dimensions is 60 ft. If the dog is in the center of the yard, the maximum length allowed for the leash is 60/2 = 30 ft.

21. The diameter of the cut piece = diameter of entire pipe = 5"

22. [($15.00)(1)+($12.60)(2)+($10.50)(4)+($7.50)(10)]/17 = $157.20/17 9.25 (closest answer in answer key is $9.30).

23. .125 + .25 + .375 + .0625 = .8125 = 13/16

24. Let x = annual pay. Then, x/26 = pay every two weeks, whereas pay every half month. His

increase is $\dfrac{x}{24} - \dfrac{x}{26} = \dfrac{x}{312}$, which represents a fractional increase of $\dfrac{x}{312} / \dfrac{x}{26} = \dfrac{1}{12}$

25. The number of different license tags = (26)(26)(10)(10)(10) = 676,000 (closest answer in answer key is 675,000).

————

TEST 2

DIRECTIONS: Each question or incomplete statement is followed by several suggested answers or completions. Select the one that BEST answers the question or completes the statement. *PRINT THE LETTER OF THE CORRECT ANSWER IN THE SPACE AT THE RIGHT.*

1. If cast iron weighs 450 pounds per cubic foot, the weight of a solid cast iron manhole cover 2 feet in diameter and 1 inch thick is MOST NEARLY _____ pounds.

   A. 94   B. 118   C. 136   D. 164

   1.____

2. The sum of 2 5/8, 3 3/16, 1 1/2, and 4 1/4 is

   A. 9 13/16   B. 10 7/16   C. 11 9/16   D. 13 3/16

   2.____

3. A pump is able to fill a tank holding 15,000 gallons in 2 hours and 30 minutes. Pumping at the same rate, an empty 60,000 gallon tank can be filled in

   A. 10 hours   B. 10 hours, 30 minutes
   C. 11 hours   D. 11 hours, 30 minutes

   3.____

4. Assume you want to add 10,000 gallons of water to a tank. If you pump water into the tank at the rate of 100 gallons per minute for one hour and 50 gallons per minute after the first hour, the total time required to add the 10,000 gallons is MOST NEARLY

   A. 1 hour, 20 minutes   B. 2 hours
   C. 2 hours, 20 minutes   D. 3 hours

   4.____

5. A tank 25 feet long, 15 feet wide, and 10 feet deep is enlarged by extending the length another 25 feet.
   The enlarged tank will be able to hold _____ more than the original tank.

   A. 50%   B. 100%   C. 150%   D. 200%

   5.____

6. If cast iron weighs 450 pounds per cubic foot, the weight of a solid cast iron manhole cover 4 feet in diameter and 1 inch thick is MOST NEARLY _____ pounds.

   A. 188   B. 236   C. 328   D. 471

   6.____

7. If four men work seven hours during the day, the number of man-hours of work done is

   A. 4   B. 7   C. 11   D. 28

   7.____

8. If it takes four men fourteen days to do a certain job, seven men working at the same rate should be able to do the same job in _____ days.

   A. 8   B. 7   C. 6   D. 5

   8.____

9. A truck leaves the garage at 9:26 A.M. and returns the same day at 3:43 P.M. The period of time that the truck was away from the garage is MOST NEARLY _____ hours, _____ minutes.

   A. 5; 17   B. 5; 43   C. 6; 17   D. 6; 26

   9.____

10. Assume that it takes 6 men 8 days to do a certain job. Working at the same speed, the number of days that it will take 4 men to do this job is

    10.____

    A. 9   B. 10   C. 12   D. 14

11. The sum of 3 5/8 + 4 1/4 + 6 1/2 + 7 1/8 is

    11.____

    A. 20 7/8   B. 21 1/4   C. 21 1/2   D. 22 1/8

12. The fraction which is equal to .0625 is

    12.____

    A. 1/64   B. 3/64   C. 1/16   D. 5/8

13. The volume, in cubic feet, of a rectangular coal bin 8 feet long by 5 feet wide by 7 feet high is MOST NEARLY

    13.____

    A. 40   B. 56   C. 186   D. 280

14. Assume that a car travels at a constant speed of 36 miles per hour.
The speed of this car, in feet per second, is MOST NEARLY (one mile equals 5,280 ft.)

    14.____

    A. 3   B. 24.6   C. 52.8   D. 879.8

15. If one-third of a 19-foot length of lumber is cut off, the length of the remaining piece will measure APPROXIMATELY

    15.____

    A. 8'8"   B. 9'8"   C. 12'8"   D. 13'8"

16. The circumference of a circle having a diameter of 10" is MOST NEARLY _____ inches.

    16.____

    A. 3.14   B. 18.72   C. 24.96   D. 31.4

17. Assume that in the purchase of paint, the seller quotes a discount of 10%.
If the price per gallon is $19.05, the actual payment, in dollars per gallon, is MOST NEARLY

    17.____

    A. $17.15   B. $17.85   C. $18.75   D. $19.50

18. Assume that a cubic foot of water contains 7 1/2 gallons. The number of gallons of water which could be contained in a rectangular tank 3 feet long, 2 feet wide, and 2 feet deep is MOST NEARLY

    18.____

    A. 12   B. 45   C. 90   D. 120

19. The volume, in cubic feet, of a slab of concrete that is 5'0" wide, 6'0" long, and 0'6" in depth is MOST NEARLY

    19.____

    A. 15.0   B. 13.5   C. 12.0   D. 10.5

20. The sum of the following pipe lengths, 22 1/8", 7 3/4", 19 7/16", and 43 5/8", is

    20.____

    A. 91 7/8"   B. 92 1/16"   C. 92 1/2"   D. 92 15/16"

21. The area, in square feet, of a plant floor that is 42 feet wide and 75 feet long is

    21.____

    A. 3,150   B. 3,100   C. 3.075   D. 2,760

22. The sum of the following dimensions, 1 5/8, 2 1/4, 4 1/16, and 3 3/16, is

    22.____

    A. 10 15/16   B. 11   C. 11 1/8   D. 11 1/4

23. Assume that six men, working together at the same rate of speed, can complete a cer-   23.____
tain job in 3 hours.
If, however, there were only four men available to do this job, and they all worked at the
same rate of speed, to complete this job would take MOST NEARLY _____ hours.

   A. 4 1/4   B. 4 1/2   C. 4 3/4   D. 5

24. Due to unforeseen difficulties, a job which would normally take 17 hours to complete was   24.____
actually completed in 21 hours.
This represents a percent increase over the normal time of MOST NEARLY

   A. 19%   B. 2.4%   C. 24%   D. 124%

25. Truck A costs $30,000 and gets 12 mpg and truck B costs $35,000 and gets 15 mpg.   25.____
After 1 year driving 12,000 miles, how much would be saved by purchasing truck A if
gasoline costs $1.50 per gallon?

   A. $1,000   B. $3,000   C. $4,700   D. $6,000

KEY (CORRECT ANSWERS)

1. B		11. C	
2. C		12. C	
3. A		13. D	
4. C		14. C	
5. B		15. C	
6. D		16. D	
7. D		17. A	
8. A		18. C	
9. C		19. A	
10. C		20. D	

21. A
22. C
23. B
24. C
25. C

SOLUTIONS TO PROBLEMS

1. $(450)(\pi)(1)^2(1/12) \approx 118$ pounds. (Note: $V = \pi R^2 H$)

2. $2\ 5/8 + 3\ 3/16 + 1\ 1/2 + 4\ 1/4 = 10\ 25/16 = 11\ 9/16$

3. To fill a 60,000 gallon tank would require $(4)(2\ 1/2\ \text{hrs.}) = 10$ hrs.

4. After 1 hour, $(100)(60) = 6000$ gallons have been added. To add the remaining 4000 gallons will require $4000 \div 50 = 80$ minutes $= 1$ hour 20 minutes. Thus, total time needed is 2 hrs. 20 min.

5. The original volume $= (25)(15)(10) = 3750$ cu.ft., and the new volume $= (50)(15)(10) = 7500$ cu.ft. The increased volume of 3750 represents an increase of $(3750/3750)(100) = 100\%$.

6. $(450)(\pi)(2)^2(1/12) \approx 471$ pounds

7. $(4)(7) = 28$ man-hours

8. $(4)(14) = 56$ man-days. Then, $56 \div 7 = 8$ days

9. From 9:26 A.M. to 3:43 P.M. $= 6$ hrs. 17 min.

10. $(6)(8) = 48$ man-days. Then, $48 \div 4 = 12$ days

11. $3\ 5/8 + 4\ 1/4 + 6\ 1/2 + 7\ 1/8 = 20\ 12/8 = 21\ 1/2$

12. $.0625 = 625/10{,}000 = 1/16$

13. $(8)(5)(7) = 280$ cu.ft.

14. $(36)(5280) = 190{,}080$ ft. per hour. Since there are 3600 seconds in 1 hour, the speed $= 190{,}080 \div 3600 = 52.8$ ft. per second.

15. $19' - 1/3(19') = 12\ 2/3, = 12'8''$

16. Circumference $= (\pi)(10'')\ 31.4''$

17. $(\$19.05)(.90) \approx \$17.15$

18. $(7\ 1/2)(3)(2)(2) = 90$ gallons

19. $(5)(6)(1/2) = 15$ cu.ft.

20. $22\ 1/8'' + 7\ 3/4'' + 19\ 7/16'' + 43\ 5/8'' = 91\ 31/16'' = 92\ 15/16''$

21. Area $= (42)(75) = 3150$ sq.ft.

22. 1 5/8 + 2 1/4 + 4 1/16 + 3 3/16 = 10 18/16 = 11 1/8

23. (6) (3) = 18 man-hours. Then, 18 / 4 = 4 1/2 hours

24. 21 - 17 = 4. Then, 4/17 ≈ 24%

25. For Truck A, the expenses are $30,000 + (1000)($1.50) = $31,500 For Truck B, the expenses are $35,000 + (800)($1.50) = $36,200. $36,200 - $31,500 = $4,700

———————

TEST 3

DIRECTIONS: Each question or incomplete statement is followed by several suggested answers or completions. Select the one that BEST answers the question or completes the statement. *PRINT THE LETTER OF THE CORRECT ANSWER IN THE SPACE AT THE RIGHT.*

1. Assume that a light maintainer and his helper replaced 25 lamps on one round of their assigned territory.
   If it took two hours to complete this round, and the maintainer's pay rate was $9.60 per hour and the helper's rate was $8.40 per hour, the labor cost of replacing each burned out lamp averaged _____ cents.

   A. 18   B. 36   C. 72   D. 144   1.____

2. A certain power distribution job will require two main-tainers at $16.00 per hour and two helpers at $13.20 per hour. The job will take three 8-hour days to complete and will require 6 hours of planning and supervision by a foreman at $19.60 per hour.
   The TOTAL labor cost for this job is

   A. $264.80   B. $501.60   C. $818.40   D. $1,519.20   2.____

3. Two identical containers are partly filled with bolts and weigh 40 lbs. and 75 lbs., respectively. To save storage space, all the bolts are put in one of the containers. The two containers now weigh 5 lbs. and 110 lbs., respectively.
   If three bolts weigh 1/2 lb., the TOTAL number of bolts is

   A. 210   B. 450   C. 630   D. 660   3.____

4. The sum of the following dimensions, 2'7 1/2", 1'8 1/2", 2'1/16", and 3/4", is   4.____

   A. 5'15 9/16"   B. 5'15 11/16"
   C. 5'7/16"   D. 6'4 9/16"

5. If a 3-foot length of contact rail weighs 150 pounds, then 39 feet of contact rail weighs _____ pounds.   5.____

   A. 1,850   B. 1,900   C. 1,950   D. 2,000

6. The sum of the following dimensions, 3'2 1/2", 8 7/8", 2'6 3/8", 2'9 3/4", and 1'0", is   6.____

   A. 9'3 1/4"   B. 10'3 1/4"   C. 10'7 1/4"   D. 16'7 1/4"

7. If a drawing for a contact rail installation is made to a scale of 1 1/2" to the foot, the drawing is said to be one _____ size.   7.____

   A. sixteenth   B. eight   C. quarter   D. half

8. If a drawing has a scale of 1/4" = 1', a dimension of 1 3/4" on the drawing would be equal to   8.____

   A. 4'   B. 5'   C. 6'   D. 7'

9. A reel weighs 600 lbs. when fully loaded with cable and 200 lbs. when empty.
   If the cable weighs 2.5 lbs. per foot, the number of reels a foreman should order for a job requiring 700 feet of this cable is _____ reels.   9.____

   A. 2   B. 3   C. 4   D. 5

10. If the scale on a working drawing is shown as 1/4" = 1', a scaled measurement of 4 1/2   10.____
    inches represents an actual length of _____ feet.

    A. 8   B. 9   C. 16   D. 18

11. A gap on the third rail starts at a subway column marked 217+79. The gap extends 68   11.____
    feet to another column marked 217+11.
    A column midway between these columns would be marked 217+_____

    A. 34   B. 39   C. 45   D. 68

12. Assume a foreman decided that 100 contact rail ties need replacing. Each tie measures   12.____
    9' x 6" x 8".
    In providing room for storing these ties at the job site, the MINIMUM storage volume
    required is APPROXIMATELY _____ cubic feet.

    A. 300   B. 360   C. 432   D. 576

13. Assume a certain job was done a year ago and took 8 men a total of 5 days to complete.   13.____
    The records show that each day involved 5 hours of overtime for half the men. Your
    assistant supervisor now assigns you the identical job to be done using 6 men and no
    overtime.
    The MINIMUM number of regular work days that should be scheduled for this job is
    _____ days.

    A. 13   B. 11   C. 9   D. 6

14. The sum of the following dimensions, 12'11 3/16", 9'8 5/8", 7'3 3/4", 5'2 1/2", and 3'1 1/   14.____
    4", is

    A. 39'5 9/16"   B. 38'3 5/16"
    C. 36'2 3/8"   D. 35'1 7/8"

15. If the scale on a drawing is 1/4" to the foot, then a 5/8" measurement would represent an   15.____
    actual length of

    A. 5'4"   B. 4'8"   C. 2'6"   D. 1'3"

16. The sum of 1 9/16", 3 1/2", 7 3/8", 10 3/4", and 12 5/8" is   16.____

    A. 33 11/16"   B. 34 13/16"   C. 35 11/16"   D. 35 13/16"

17. A reel containing an unknown length of cable weighs 340 pounds.   17.____
    If the empty reel weighs 119 lbs. and the cable weighs 0.85 lb. per foot, the number of
    feet of cable on the reel is

    A. 140   B. 260   C. 400   D. 540

18. If the scale on a shop drawing is 1/4" to the foot, then a part which measures 3 3/8 inches   18.____
    long on the drawing has an actual length of_____ feet _____ inches.

    A. 12; 6   B. 13; 6   C. 13; 9   D. 14; 9

19. Taking into account time and one-half payment for time over 40 hours of work, the gross   19.____
    pay of an employee who works 43 hours in a week at a rate of pay of $5.34 per hour is

    A. $213.60   B. $229.62   C. $237.63   D. $245.64

20. The sum of 0.365 + 3.941 + 10.676 + 0.784 is

    A. 13.766   B. 15.666   C. 15.756   D. 15.766

20.____

21. An air conditioning unit is rated at 1000 watts. The unit is run for 10 hours per day, five days per week. If the cost for electrical energy is 50 cents per kilowatt-hour, the weekly cost for electricity should be

    A. $2.50   B. $5.00   C. $25.00   D. $250.00

21.____

22. Assume that the cost of a certain wiring installation is broken down as follows: Materials $1,200, Labor $800, and Rental of equipment $400.
The percentage of the total cost of the job that can be charged to Labor is MOST NEARLY

    A. 12.3   B. 33.3   C. 40.0   D. 66.6

22.____

23. Assume that it takes 4 electrician's helpers 6 days to do a certain job.
Working at the same rate of speed, the number of days it will take 3 electrician's helpers to do the same job is

    A. 6   B. 7   C. 8   D. 9

23.____

24. Assume that a 120-volt, 25-cycle magnetic coil is to be rewound to operate properly on 60-cycles at the same voltage.
If the coil at 25-cycles has 1,000 turns, at 60-cycles the number of turns should be MOST NEARLY

    A. 2,400   B. 1,200   C. 416   D. 208

24.____

25. A light maintainer whose rate is $14.40 per hour is assigned to replace burned-out station and tunnel lamps. During 4 hours, he replaces 28 lamps.
The average labor cost for replacing each of these burned-out lamps was NEAREST to

    A. 56¢   B. $1.04   C. $2.00   D. $3.60

25.____

KEY (CORRECT ANSWERS)

1.	D	11.	C
2.	D	12.	A
3.	C	13.	C
4.	D	14.	B
5.	C	15.	C
6.	B	16.	D
7.	B	17.	B
8.	D	18.	B
9.	D	19.	C
10.	D	20.	D

21.	C
22.	B
23.	C
24.	C
25.	C

SOLUTIONS TO PROBLEMS

1. (2)($9.60+$8.40) = $36.00. Then, $36.00 ÷ 25 = $1.44 or 144 cents.

2. (2)($16.00)(24) + (2)($13.20)(24) + (6)($19.60) = $1519.20

3. An empty container weighs 5 lbs., so the container which contains bolts and weighs 110 lbs. actually has 105 lbs. of bolts. Since 3 bolts weigh 1/2 lb., 105 lbs. would contain (105/1/2)(3) = 630 bolts.

4. 2'7 1/4" + 1'8 1/2" + 2'1/16" + 3/4" = 5'15 25/16" = 6 '4 9/16"

5. 39 feet of rail weighs (13)(150) = 1950 pounds

6. 3'2 1/4" + 8 7/8" + 2'6 3/8" + 2'9 3/4" + 1'0" = 8'25 18/8" = 10'3 1/4"

7. 1 1/2"/1" = 3/2.1/12=1/8

8. I 3/4" ÷ 1/4" = 7 Then, (7)(1') = 7'

9. 600 - 200 = 400. Then, 400 ÷ 2.5 = 160 ft. of cable per reel. Since 700 ft. of cable is needed, 700/160 = 4.375, which means 5 reels will be required (must round up).

10. 4 1/2" ÷ 1/4" = 9/2 4/1 = 18 Then, (18)(1') = 18'

11. Half of 68 = 34; 11 + 34 = 45; 79 - 34 = 45

12. (100)(9')(1/2')(2/3') = 300 cu.ft.

13. Number of man-days = (4)(5) + (4)(5)(1 5/8) =52.5
    For 6 men working only 8-hour days, 52.5 ÷ 6 = 8.75 = 9 days needed.

14. 12'11 3/16" + 9'8 5/8" + 7'3 3/4" + 5'2 1/2" + 3'1 1/4" = 36'25 37/16" = 38'3 5/16"

15. 5/8" ÷ 1/4" = 5/8 . 4/1 = 2 1/2. Then, (2 1/2)(1') = 2'6"

16. 1 9/16" + 3 1/2" + 7 3/8" + 10 3/4" + 12 5/8" = 33 45/16" = 35 13/36"

17. 340 - 119 = 221 lbs. Then, 221 ÷ .85 = 260 ft.

18. 3 3/8" ÷ 1/4" = 27/8 . 4/1 = 13/ 1/2. Then, (13 1/2) (1') = 13 ft. 6 in.

19. (40)($5.34) + (3)($5.34)(1.5) = $237.63

20. 0.365 +3.941 + 10.676 + 0.784 = 15.766

21. (1000)(10)(5) = 50,000 watt-hours = 50 kilowatt-hours. Then, (50)($.50) = $25.00

22. $800 / ($1200+$800+$400) =1/3 ≈ 33.3%

23. (4)(6) = 24. Then, 24/ 3 = 8 days

24. Let x = number of required turns. Since the number of cycles varies inversely as the number of turns, 25/60 = x/1000.
Solving, x 416 (actually 416 2/3)

25. ($14.40)(4) = $57.60. Then, $57.60 ÷ 28 ≈ $2.06

PREPARING WRITTEN MATERIAL

PARAGRAPH REARRANGEMENT
COMMENTARY

The sentences which follow are in scrambled order. You are to rearrange them in proper order and indicate the letter choice containing the correct answer at the space at the right.

Each group of sentences in this section is actually a paragraph presented in scrambled order. Each sentence in the group has a place in that paragraph; no sentence is to be left out. You are to read each group of sentences and decide upon the best order in which to put the sentences so as to form as well-organized paragraph.

The questions in this section measure the ability to solve a problem when all the facts relevant to its solution are not given.

More specifically, certain positions of responsibility and authority require the employee to discover connections between events sometimes, apparently, unrelated. In order to do this, the employee will find it necessary to correctly infer that unspecified events have probably occurred or are likely to occur. This ability becomes especially important when action must be taken on incomplete information.

Accordingly, these questions require competitors to choose among several suggested alternatives, each of which presents a different sequential arrangement of the events. Competitors must choose the MOST logical of the suggested sequences.

In order to do so, they may be required to draw on general knowledge to infer missing concepts or events that are essential to sequencing the given events. Competitors should be careful to infer only what is essential to the sequence. The plausibility of the wrong alternatives will always require the inclusion of unlikely events or of additional chains of events which are NOT essential to sequencing the given events.

It's very important to remember that you are looking for the best of the four possible choices, and that the best choice of all may not even be one of the answers you're given to choose from.

There is no one right way to solve these problems. Many people have found it helpful to first write out the order of the sentences, as they would have arranged them, on their scrap paper before looking at the possible answers. If their optimum answer is there, this can save them some time. If it isn't, this method can still give insight into solving the problem. Others find it most helpful to just go through each of the possible choices, contrasting each as they go along. You should use whatever method feels comfortable, and works, for you.

While most of these types of questions are not that difficult, we've added a higher percentage of the difficult type, just to give you more practice. Usually there are only one or two questions on this section that contain such subtle distinctions that you're unable to answer confidently, and you then may find yourself stuck deciding between two possible choices, neither of which you're sure about.

———

EXAMINATION SECTION
TEST 1

DIRECTIONS: The sentences that follow are in scrambled order. You are to rearrange them in proper order and indicate the letter choice containing the correct answer. *PRINT THE LETTER OF THE CORRECT ANSWER IN THE SPACE AT THE RIGHT.*

1. Below are four statements labeled W., X., Y., and Z.   1.____
    W. He was a strict and fanatic drillmaster.
    X. The word is always used in a derogatory sense and generally shows resent-
        ment and anger on the part of the user.
    Y. It is from the name of this Frenchman that we derive our English word, martinet.
    Z. Jean Martinet was the Inspector-General of Infantry during the reign of King
        Louis XIV.
   The *PROPER* order in which these sentences should be placed in a paragraph is:

    A. X, Z, W, Y   B. X, Z, Y, W   C. Z, W, Y, X   D. Z, Y, W, X

2. In the following paragraph, the sentences which are numbered, have been jumbled.   2.____
    1. Since then it has undergone changes.
    2. It was incorporated in 1955 under the laws of the State of New York.
    3. Its primary purpose, a cleaner city, has, however, remained the same.
    4. The Citizens Committee works in cooperation with the Mayor's Inter-departmen-
        tal Committee for a Clean City.
   The order in which these sentences should be arranged to form a well-organized paragraph is:

    A. 2, 4, 1, 3   B. 3, 4, 1, 2   C. 4, 2, 1, 3   D. 4, 3, 2, 1

Questions 3-5.

DIRECTIONS: The sentences listed below are part of a meaningful paragraph but they are not given in their proper order. You are to decide what would be the *best order* in which to put the sentences so as to form a well-organized paragraph. Each sentence has a place in the paragraph; there are no extra sentences. You are then to answer questions 3 to 5 inclusive on the basis of your rearrangements of these scrambled sentences into a properly organized paragraph.

In 1887 some insurance companies organized an Inspection Department to advise their clients on all phases of fire prevention and protection. Probably this has been due to the smaller annual fire losses in Great Britain than in the United States. It tests various fire prevention devices and appliances and determines manufacturing hazards and their safeguards. Fire research began earlier in the United States and is more advanced than in Great Britain. Later they established a laboratory specializing in electrical, mechanical, hydraulic, and chemical fields.

3. When the five sentences are arranged in proper order, the paragraph starts with the sentence which begins   3.____

    A. "In 1887..."   B. "Probably this ..."   C. "It tests ..."
    D. "Fire research ..."   E. "Later they ..."

4. In the last sentence listed above, "they" refers to   4.____

    A. insurance companies
    B. the United States and Great Britain
    C. the Inspection Department
    D. clients
    E. technicians

5. When the above paragraph is properly arranged, it ends with the words   5.____

    A. "... and protection."   B. "... the United States."
    C. "... their safeguards."   D. "... in Great Britain."
    E. "... chemical fields."

_____

KEY (CORRECT ANSWERS)

1. C
2. C
3. D
4. A
5. C

_____

TEST 2

DIRECTIONS: In each of the questions numbered 1 through 5, several sentences are given. For each question, choose as your answer the group of numbers that represents the *most logical* order of these sentences if they were arranged in paragraph form. *PRINT THE LETTER OF THE CORRECT ANSWER IN THE SPACE AT THE RIGHT.*

1. 1. It is established when one shows that the landlord has prevented the tenant's enjoyment of his interest in the property leased.
    2. Constructive eviction is the result of a breach of the covenant of quiet enjoyment implied in all leases.
    3. In some parts of the United States, it is not complete until the tenant vacates within a reasonable time.
    4. Generally, the acts must be of such serious and permanent character as to deny the tenant the enjoyment of his possessing rights.
    5. In this event, upon abandonment of the premises, the tenant's liability for that ceases.

    The CORRECT answer is:

    A. 2, 1, 4, 3, 5   B. 5, 2, 3, 1, 4   C. 4, 3, 1, 2, 5
    D. 1, 3, 5, 4, 2

    1.____

2. 1. The powerlessness before private and public authorities that is the typical experience of the slum tenant is reminiscent of the situation of blue-collar workers all through the nineteenth century.
    2. Similarly, in recent years, this chapter of history has been reopened by anti-poverty groups which have attempted to organize slum tenants to enable them to bargain collectively with their landlords about the conditions of their tenancies.
    3. It is familiar history that many of the workers remedied their condition by joining together and presenting their demands collectively.
    4. Like the workers, tenants are forced by the conditions of modern life into substantial dependence on these who possess great political arid economic power.
    5. What's more, the very fact of dependence coupled with an absence of education and self-confidence makes them hesitant and unable to stand up for what they need from those in power.

    The CORRECT answer is:

    A. 5, 4, 1, 2, 3   B. 2, 3, 1, 5, 4   C. 3, 1, 5, 4, 2
    D. 1, 4, 5, 3, 2

    2.____

3. 1. A railroad, for example, when not acting as a common carrier may contract away responsibility for its own negligence.
    2. As to a landlord, however, no decision has been found relating to the legal effect of a clause shifting the statutory duty of repair to the tenant.
    3. The courts have not passed on the validity of clauses relieving the landlord of this duty and liability.
    4. They have, however, upheld the validity of exculpatory clauses in other types of contracts.
    5. Housing regulations impose a duty upon the landlord to maintain leased premises in safe condition.

    3.____

6. As another example, a bailee may limit his liability except for gross negligence, willful acts, or fraud.

The CORRECT answer is:

A. 2, 1, 6, 4, 3, 5   B. 1, 3, 4, 5, 6, 2   C. 3, 5, 1, 4, 2, 6
D. 5, 3, 4, 1, 6, 2

4. 1. Since there are only samples in the building, retail or consumer sales are generally eschewed by mart occupants, and in some instances, rigid controls are maintained to limit entrance to the mart only to those persons engaged in retailing.
    2. Since World War I, in many larger cities, there has developed a new type of property, called the mart building.
    3. It can, therefore, be used by wholesalers and jobbers for the display of sample merchandise.
    4. This type of building is most frequently a multi-storied, finished interior property which is a cross between a retail arcade and a loft building.
    5. This limitation enables the mart occupants to ship the orders from another location after the retailer or dealer makes his selection from the samples.

4.____

The CORRECT answer is:

A. 2, 4, 3, 1, 5   B. 4, 3, 5, 1, 2   C. 1, 3, 2, 4, 5
D. 1, 4, 2, 3, 5

5. 1. In general, staff-line friction reduces the distinctive contribution of staff personnel.
    2. The conflicts, however, introduce an uncontrolled element into the managerial system.
    3. On the other hand, the natural resistance of the line to staff innovations probably usefully restrains over-eager efforts to apply untested procedures on a large scale.
    4. Under such conditions, it is difficult to know when valuable ideas are being sacrificed.
    5. The relatively weak position of staff, requiring accommodation to the line, tends to restrict their ability to engage in free, experimental innovation.

5.____

The CORRECT answer is:

A. 4, 2, 3, 1, 3   B. 1, 5, 3, 2, 4   C. 5, 3, 1, 2, 4
D. 2, 1, 4, 5, 3

KEY (CORRECT ANSWERS)

1. A
2. D
3. D
4. A
5. B

TEST 3

DIRECTIONS: Questions 1 through 4 consist of six sentences which can be arranged in a logical sequence. For each question, select the choice which places the numbered sentences in the *most logical* sequence. *PRINT THE LETTER OF THE CORRECT ANSWER IN THE SPACE AT THE RIGHT.*

1.   1. The burden of proof as to each issue is determined before trial and remains upon the same party throughout the trial.
    2. The jury is at liberty to believe one witness' testimony as against a number of contradictory witnesses.
    3. In a civil case, the party bearing the burden of proof is required to prove his contention by a fair preponderance of the evidence.
    4. However, it must be noted that a fair preponderance of evidence does not necessarily mean a greater number of witnesses.
    5. The burden of proof is the burden which rests upon one of the parties to an action to persuade the trier of the facts, generally the jury, that a proposition he asserts is true.
    6. If the evidence is equally balanced, or if it leaves the jury in such doubt as to be unable to decide the controversy either way, judgment must be given against the party upon whom the burden of proof rests.

The CORRECT answer is:

A. 3, 2, 5, 4, 1, 6   B. 1, 2, 6, 5, 3, 4   C. 3, 4, 5, 1, 2, 6
D. 5, 1, 3, 6, 4, 2

1.____

2.   1. If a parent is without assets and is unemployed, he cannot be convicted of the crime of non-support of a child.
    2. The term "sufficient ability" has been held to mean sufficient financial ability.
    3. It does not matter if his unemployment is by choice or unavoidable circumstances.
    4. If he fails to take any steps at all, he may be liable to prosecution for endangering the welfare of a child.
    5. Under the penal law, a parent is responsible for the support of his minor child only if the parent is "of sufficient ability."
    6. An indigent parent may meet his obligation by borrowing money or by seeking aid under the provisions of the Social Welfare Law.

The CORRECT answer is:

A. 6, 1, 5, 3, 2, 4   B. 1, 3, 5, 2, 4, 6   C. 5, 2, 1, 3, 6, 4
D. 1, 6, 4, 5, 2, 3

2.____

3. 1. Consider, for example, the case of a rabble rouser who urges a group of twenty people to go out and break the windows of a nearby factory.
   2. Therefore, the law fills the indicated gap with the crime of inciting to riot.
   3. A person is considered guilty of inciting to riot when he urges ten or more persons to engage in tumultuous and violent conduct of a kind likely to create public alarm.
   4. However, if he has not obtained the cooperation of at least four people, he cannot be charged with unlawful assembly.
   5. The charge of inciting to riot was added to the law to cover types of conduct which cannot be classified as either the crime of "riot" or the crime of "unlawful assembly."
   6. If he acquires the acquiescence of at least four of them, he is guilty of unlawful assembly even if the project does not materialize.

   The CORRECT answer is:

   A. 3, 5, 1, 6, 4, 2   B. 5, 1, 4, 6, 2, 3   C. 3, 4, 1, 5, 2, 6
   D. 5, 1, 4, 6, 3, 2

3.____

4. 1. If, however, the rebuttal evidence presents an issue of credibility, it is for the jury to determine whether the presumption has, in fact, been destroyed.
   2. Once sufficient evidence to the contrary is introduced, the presumption disappears from the trial.
   3. The effect of a presumption is to place the burden upon the adversary to come forward with evidence to rebut the presumption.
   4. When a presumption is overcome and ceases to exist in the case, the fact or facts which gave rise to the presumption still remain.
   5. Whether a presumption has been overcome is ordinarily a question for the court.
   6. Such information may furnish a basis for a logical inference.

   The CORRECT answer is:

   A. 4, 6, 2, 5, 1, 3   B. 3, 2, 5, 1, 4, 6   C. 5, 3, 6, 4, 2, 1
   D. 5, 4, 1, 2, 6, 3

4.____

KEY (CORRECT ANSWERS)

1. D
2. C
3. A
4. B

BASIC INFORMATION ON POLLUTION AND POLLUTANTS

CONTENTS

BASIC INFORMATION ON POLLUTION AND POLLUTANTS

Following Is background information on noise, water , air and pesticide-herbicide pollution, and on the recycling process through which students and other members of the community can take individual action against pollution.

I. NOISE

A. Decibel levels

The following are averages:

Shout - 90	Motorcycle - 110
Normal conversation - 50-60	Riveting gun - 130
Whisper - 20	Thunderclap - 120
Jet - 117	

B. Health

It has been shown in animal studies, however, that rats born of mothers exposed to noise pollution during pregnancy had more difficulty in learning maze patterns than rats born of unstressed mother

Well-informed scientists reckon that if city noise continues to rise as it is presently rising, by one decibel a year, everyone will be stone deaf by the year 2000.

Rats, under prolonged noise exposure, have turned homosexual.

Dr. D. Glass (NYU) and Dr. J.Singer (SUNY) have shown that repeated random and unpredictable noises produce irritation and frustration, as well as dramatic declines in work efficiency even after the noise is stopped. Their studies disproved the popular assumption that man can learn to adjust to almost any noise.

C. Costs

Silence seems to cost between 5 and 10 percent more on most products.

II. PESTICIDES/HERBICIDES

A. General

Elimination of the use of persistent toxic pesticides should be t he goal.

B. Definition

Persistent, toxic pesticides include the following:

DDT	Chlordane
Aldrin	Lindane
Endrin	Benzene
Heptachlor	Hexachloride
Texaphene	Dieldrin

and there are those chlorinated hydrocarbons that do not break down completely in a few days or even a few years into less harmful materials. Of pesticides, all are not persistent. All, however, are questionable.

C. Wildlife

It has been discovered that many forms of wildlife - brown pelicans, peregrine falcons, and bald eagles, to name a few --
(1) have large quantities of DDT In their systems, and eggs, and
(2) are, in some areas, no longer capable of reproducing.

D. DDT

DDT Is an active product in over 35 products.

Evidence of severe oceanic contamination is the fact that some seabirds which never approach land except to nest are sometimes more contaminated with DDT than land birds.

E. Sea Creatures

Some organisms are unbelievably sensitive to the chlorinated hydrocarbons. For instance, nearly half the population of brine shrimp is killed within three weeks at a concentration of one part per trillion DDT, or 1/1000 of a drop in a tank-car lot. Temperature-control mechanisms are upset in young salmon at a few parts per billion, and death in a natural competitive environment could easily be the result.

III. WATER POLLUTION

A. Eutrophication

Eutrophication is a process whereby nutrients (nitrates and phosphates) are added to the water in bodies of water, causing multiplication of algae and small bacterial plants, which, due to their numbers, die in huge quantities, and exhaust the oxygen supply in decomposition. The water's oxygen is depleted to the extent that all other forms of life are choked to death.

Very recently the soap and detergent industry contended that because it is not the only cause of lake eutrophication, it should not be asked to find substitutes for phosphates in its detergents.

B. Phosphates

Phosphates are nutrients found in many detergents in the follow-ing concentrations:

Axion (Colgate Palmolive)	- 3%
Biz (Procter and Gamble)	- 40.4%
Bio-Ad (Colgate)	- 35.5%
Salvo (Procter and Gamble)	- 30.71%
Oxydol(Procter and Gamble)	- 30.7%

Tide (Procter and Gamble)	- 30.6%
Bold (Procter and Gamble)	- 30.25%
Ajax Laundry (Colgate)	- 25.2%
Punch (Colgate)	- 25.8%
Drive (Lever)	- 25.3%
Dreft (Procter and Gamble)	- 24.5%
Gain (Procter and Gamble)	- 23.1%
Duz (Procter and Gamble)	- 23.15%
Bonus (Procter and Gamble)	- 22.3%
Breeze (Lever)	- 22.2%
Cheer (Procter and Gamble)	- 22.05
Fab (Colgate)	- 21.5%
Cold Power (Colgate)	- 19.9%
Cold Water All (Lever)	- 8.8%
Wisk (Lever)	- 7.6%
Diaper Pure (Boyle)	- 5.0%
Trend (Purex)	- 1.4%

(A low-phosphate product, some say, does not get clothes clean. The answer is to add a"water softener" to the wash, and performanc is good.)

C. Fish

Over 15 million fish died last year from water pollution.

D. Fire

The Cuyahoga River, because of the general irresponsibility of polluters, was so contaminated with flammable oil and petroleum byproducts, that it caught on fire.

IV. AIR POLLUTION

A. General

According to the U.S. Public Health Service, any community with a population of 50,000 or more, has a real problem with air pollution.

The effects of air pollution are directly experienced by the wore than half of our population liing in our great widespread urban-suburban cornplexes .

B. Cancer

It has been generally concluded that air pollution is one of the factors contributing to the steady increase of lung cancer.

According to the U.S. Public Health Service, skin cancer that developed on a mouse after its skin was painted with pollutants from urban air, was probably caused by those pollutants.

C. Smoking

A person breathing the city's air inhales as much benzopyrene, a cancer-inducing hydrocarbon, as he would if he smoked two packs of cigarettes a day.

D. Trees

Early in this century, fumes from smelting operations in the Duektown-Copper Hill area of Southeastern Tennessee virtually de-nunded 17,000 acres (27 sq. miles) of forest land and severely damagec another 30,000 acres. Much of the area, bare and eroded still, has been likened by a recent observer to "the back side of the Moon."

During the summer of 1969, Christmas tree plantations along the Maryland-West Virginia border suffered heavy foliage damage. Plant scientists are convinced that air pollution was the cause and a nearby power-generating station was the source of the trouble.

E. Breathing

Each breath you take carries some 40,000 particles of dust if you are surrounded by "clean country air, some 70,000 if you live in the city. Then come the noxious gases. The nation's cars daily release: 250,000 tons of carbon monoxide, 16,500 to 33,000 tons of hydrocarbons, and 4,000 to 12,000 tons of nitrogen oxides.

F. Industry

The burning of coal for heat and power sends 48,000 tons of sulphur dioxide into the air very day.

G. Cars

The automobile is the primary villain in air pollution. It accounts for at least 60% of the total air pollution in the U.S., 85% of the pollution in some of our sprawling urban areas.

In the United States, the automobile produces 90$ of all carbon monoxide pollution.

V. RECYCLING

Natural processes are a system of cycles. All things are *a* part of this system. When man takes natural resources to produce things, he often interrupts a cycle. The idea behind recycling is to channel an item, once used, back into the system, thereby recycling it.

Our objective is to begin to treat garbage and trash with due respect. Reduce the amount of waste you produce by considering what will happen to each thing you purchase. Packaging will play an important role here. Things like cellophane, waxed paper, styro-foam, and plastics are not bio-degradable, or easily recyclable, and should be avoided. Try and recycle all things you do not need.

When, considering recycling, first re-use the item in its original form (use a box again). If this is not possible, utilize it for its material content (sell old paper to waste-paper company), An empty garvage can is a sign of ecological living.
Here are some ideas for you to use when recycling:

A. <u>Paper</u> - Read magazines and newspapers in the library. Avoid paper towels, napkins, diapers, cupss plates. Write on both sides. Use lunch boxes instead of paper sacks. Re-use one plastic bag to wrap sandwiches, etc., in. Use popcorn or something bio-degradable to cushion shipped or mailed items.

B. <u>Bottles</u> - Purchase all bottled drinks and liquids in reusable bottles. You are paying for the "convenience" of throw-away bottles - increased disposal costs and destruction of the environment, as well as higher purchase prices. Coke costs . 85?/ fluid ounce in 16-oz. deposit bottles., and 1.02?/fluid oz. in 16-oz. one way, and 1.36? an oz. in 12-oz. aluminum cans. Ask your grocer to continue to stock deposit bottles, and return your bottles to him, or write to the National Soft Drink Association, 1128 16th Street N.W., Washington, D.C. 20036, and tell them to continue deposit bottles. A typical deposit bottle is returned about 20 times

C. <u>Cloth</u> - Give usable clothing to one of the charity organizations operating a second-hand store. Buy clothes at a secondhand store. Sell old cloth to rag companies. They usually pay about 3?/lb. The clothing industry requires a great deal of agricultural land.

D. <u>Organic Material</u> - Keep a bucket in your kitchen for your food scraps. Bury them in your yard about 6" deep so they won't attract flies or dogs. They will decompose and fertilize the soil. Grow your own food. By doing so, you completely eliminate many pack-aging and additive/pesticide/chemical problems.

GLOSSARY OF ENVIRONMENTAL TERMS

TABLE OF CONTENTS

GLOSSARY OF ENVIRONMENTAL TERMS

<u>A</u>

ABATEMENT - The method of reducing the degree or intensity of pollution, also the use of such a method.

ABSORPTION - The penetration of a substance into or through another. For example, in air pollution control, absorption is the dissolving of a soluble gas, present in an emission, in a liquid which can be extracted.

ACCELERATOR - In radiology, a device for imparting high velocity to charged particles such as electrons or protons. These fast particles can penetrate matter and are known as radiation.

ACCLIMATION - The physiological and behavioral adjustments of an organism to changes in its immediate environment.

ACCLIMATIZATION - The acclimation or adaptation of a particular species over several generations to a marked change in the environment.

ACTIVATED CARBON - A highly adsorbent form of carbon, used to remove odors and toxic substances from gaseous emissions. In advanced waste treatment, activated carbon is used to remove dissolved organic matter from waste water.

ACTIVATED SLUDGE - Sludge that has been aerated and subjected to bacterial action, used to remove organic matter from sewage.

ACTIVATED SLUDGE PROCESS - The process of using biologically active sewage sludge to hasten breakdown of organic matter in raw sewage during secondary waste treatment.

ACUTE TOXICITY - Any poisonous effect produced within a short period of time, usually up to 24-96 hours, resulting in severe biological harm and often death.

ADAPTATION - A change in structure or habit of an organism that produces better adjustment to the environment.

ADSORPTION - The adhesion of a substance to the surface of a solid or liquid. Adsorption is often used to extract pollutants by causing them to be attached to such adsorbents as activated carbon or silica gel. Hydrophobic, or water-repulsing adsorbents, are used to extract oil from waterways in oil spills.

ADULTERANTS - Chemicals or substances that by law do not belong in a food, plant, animal or pesticide formulation. Adulterated products are subject to seizure by the Food and Drug Administration.

ADVANCED WASTE TREATMENT - Waste water treatment beyond the secondary or biological stage that includes removal of nutrients such as phosphorus and nitrogen and a high percentage of suspended solids. Advanced waste treatment, known as tertiary treatment, is the *polishing stage* of waste water treatment and produces a high quality effluent.

AERATION - The process of being supplied or impregnated with air. Aeration is used in waste water treatment to foster biological and chemical purification.

AEROBIC - This refers to life or processes that can occur only in the presence of oxygen.

AEROSOL - A suspension of liquid or solid particles in the air.

AFTERBURNER - An air pollution abatement device that removes undesirable organic gases through incineration.

AGRICULTURAL POLLUTION - The liquid and solid wastes from all types of farming, including runoff from pesticides, fertilizers, and feedlots; erosion and dust from plowing animal manure and carcasses and drop residues and debris. It has been estimated that agricultural pollution in the U.S. has amounted to more than 2 1/2 billion tons per year.

AIR CURTAIN - A method for mechanical containment of oil spills. Air is bubbled through a perforated pipe causing an upward water flow that retards the spreading of oil. Air curtains are also used as barriers to prevent fish from entering a polluted body of water.

AIR MASS - A widespread body of air with properties that were established while the air was situated over a particular region of the earth's surface and that undergoes specific modification while in transit away from that region.

AIR MONITORING - (See MONITORING.)

AIR POLLUTION - The presence of contaminants in the air in concentrations that prevent the normal dispersive ability of the air and that interfere directly or indirectly with man's health, safety, or comfort or with the full use and enjoyment of his property.

AIR POLLUTION EPISODE - The occurrence of abnormally high concentrations of air pollutants usually due to low winds and temperature inversion and accompanied by an increase in illness and death. (See INVERSION.)

AIR QUALITY CONTROL REGION - An area designated by the Federal government where two or more communities - either in the same or different states - share a common air pollution problem. AIR QUALITY CRITERIA - The levels of pollution and lengths of exposure at which adverse effects on health and welfare occur.

AIR QUALITY STANDARDS - The prescribed level of pollutants in the outside air that cannot be exceeded legally during a specified time in a specified geographical area.

ALGAL BLOOM - A proliferation of living algae on the surface of lakes, streams or ponds. Algal blooms are stimulated by phosphate enrichment.

ALPHA PARTICLE - A positively charged particle emitted by certain radioactive materials. It is the least penetrating of the three common types of radiation (alpha, beta and gamma) and usually not dangerous to plants, animals, or man.

AMBIENT AIR - Any unconfined portion of the atmosphere; the outside air.

ANADROMOUS - Type of fish that ascend rivers from the sea to spawn.

ANAEROBIC - Refers to life or processes that occur in the absence of oxygen.

ANTICOAGULANT - A chemical that intereferes with blood clotting, often used as a rodenticide.

ANTI-DEGRADATION CLAUSE - A provision in air quality and water quality laws that prohibits deterioration of air or water quality in areas where the pollution levels are presently below those allowed.

AQUIFER - An underground bed or stratum of earth, gravel, or porous stone that contains water.

AQUATIC PLANTS - Plants that grow in water, either floating on the surface, growing up from the bottom of the body of water, or growing under the surface of the water.

AREA SOURCE - In air pollution, any small individual fuel combustion source, including any transportation sources. This is a general definition; area source is legally and precisely defined in Federal regulations. (See POINT SOURCE.)

ASBESTOS - A mineral fiber with countless industrial uses; a hazardous air pollutant when inhaled.

A-SCALE SOUND LEVEL - The measurement of sound approximating the auditory sensitivity of the human ear. The A-Scale sound level is used to measure the relative noisiness or annoyance of common sounds.

ASSIMILATION - Conversion or incorporation of absorbed nutrients into protoplasm. Also refers to the ability of a body of water to purify itself of organic pollution.

ATMOSPHERE - The layer of air surrounding the earth.

ATOMIC PILE - A nuclear reactor.

ATTRACTANT - A chemical or agent that lures insects or other pests by olfactory stimulation.

ATTRITION - Wearing or grinding down by friction. One of the three basic contributing processes of air pollution; the others are vaporization and combustion.

AUDIOMETER - An instrument for measuring hearing sensitivity.

AUTOTROPHIC - Self-nourishing: denoting those organisms capable of constructing organic matter from inorganic substances.

B

BACKFILL - The material used to refill a ditch or other excavation, or the process of doing so.

BACKGROUND LEVEL - With respect to air pollution, amounts of pollutants present in the ambient air due to natural sources.

BACKGROUND RADIATION - Normal radiation present in the lower atmosphere from cosmic rays and from earth sources.

BACTERIA - Single-celled microorganisms that lack chlorophyll. Some bacteria are capable of causing human, animal, or plant diseases; others are essential in pollution control because they break down organic matter in the air and in the water.

BAFFLE - Any deflector device used to change the direction of flow or the velocity of water, sewage, or products of combustion such as fly ash or coarse particulate matter. Also used in deadening sound.

BAGHOUSE - An air pollution abatement device used to trap particu-lates by filtering gas streams through large fabric bags, usually made of glass fibers.

BALING - A means of reducing the volume of solid waste by compaction.

BALLISTIC SEPARATOR - A machine that separates inorganic from organic matter in a composting process.

BAND APPLICATION - With respect to pesticides, the application of the chemical over or next to each row of plants in a field.

BAR SCREEN - In waste water treatment, a screen that removes large floating and suspended solids.

BASAL APPLICATION - With respect to pesticides, the application of the pesticide formulation on stems or trunks of plants just above the soil line.

BASIN - (See RIVER BASIN.)

BENTHIC REGION - The bottom of a body of water. This region supports the benthos, a type of life that not only lives upon, but contributes to the character of the bottom.

BENTHOS - The plant and animal life whose habitat is the bottom of a sea, lake, or river.

BERYLLIUM - A metal that when airborne has adverse effects on human health, it has been declared a hazardous air pollutant. It is primarily discharged by operations such as machine shops, ceramic and propellant plants and foundries.

BETA PARTICLE - An elementary particle emitted by radioactive decay that may cause skin burns. It is easily stopped by a thin sheet of metal.

BIOASSAY - The employment of living organisms to determine the biological effect of some substance, factor, or condition.

BIOCHEMICAL OXYGEN DEMAND (BOD) - A measure of the amount of oxygen consumed in the biological processes that break down organic matter in water. Large amounts of organic waste use up large amounts of dissolved oxygen, thus the greater the degree of pollution, the greater the BOD.

BIODEGRADABLE - The process of decomposing quickly as a result of the action of microorganisms.

BIOLOGICAL CONTROL - A method of controlling pests by means of introduced or naturally occurring predatory organisms, sterilization, or the use of inhibiting hormones, etc. rather than by mechanical or chemical means.

BIOLOGICAL OXIDATION - The process by which bacterial and other microorganisms feed on complex organic materials and decompose them. Self-purification of waterways and activated sludge and trickling filter waste water treatment processes depend on this principle. The process is also called biochemical oxidation.

BIOMONITORING - The use of living organisms to test the suitability of effluent for discharge into receiving waters and to test the quality of such waters downstream from a discharge.

BIOSPHERE - The portion of the earth and its atmosphere capable of supporting life.

BIOSTABILIZER - A machine used to convert solid waste into compost by grinding and aeration.

BIOTA - All the species of plants and animals occurring within a certain area.

BLOOM - A proliferation of living algae and/or other aquatic plants on the surface of lakes or ponds. Blooms are frequently stimulated by phosphate enrichment.

BOD - The amount of dissolved oxygen consumed in five days by biological processes breakdown of organic matter in an effluent. (See BIOCHEMICAL OXYGEN DEMAND.)

BOG - Wet, spongy land usually poorly drained, highly acid, and rich in plant residue.

BOOM - A floating device that is used to contain oil on a body of water.

BOTANICAL PESTICIDE - A plant-produced chemical used to control pests; for example, nicotine, strychnine, or orpyrethrun.

BRACKISH WATER - A mixture of fresh and salt water.

BREEDER - A nuclear reactor that produces more fuel than it consumes.

BROADCAST APPLICATION - With respect to pesticides, the application of a chemical over an entire field, lawn, or other area.

BURIAL GROUND (GRAVEYARD) - A place for burying unwanted radioactive materials to prevent radiation escape, the earth or water acting as a shield. Such materials must be placed in water-tight, noncorrodible containers so the radioactive material cannot leach out and invade underground water supplies.

C

CADMIUM - (See HEAVY METALS.)

CARBON DIOXIDE (CO_2) - A colorless, odorless, nonpoisonous gas that is a normal part of the ambient air. CO_2 is a product of fossil fuel combustion, and some researchers have theorized that excess CO_2 raises atmospheric temperatures.

CARBON MONOXIDE (CO) - A colorless, odorless, highly toxic gas that is a normal byproduct of incomplete fossil fuel combustion. CO, one of the major air pollutants, can be harmful in small amounts if breathed over a certain period of time.

CARCINOGENIC - Cancer producing.

CATALYTIC CONVERTER - An air pollution abatement device that removes organic contaminants by oxidizing them into carbon dioxide and water through chemical reaction. Can be used to reduce nitrogen oxide emissions from motor vehicles.

CAUSTIC SODA - Sodium hydroxide (NaOH), a strongly alkaline, caustic substance used as the cleaning agent in some detergents. CELLS - With respect to solid waste disposal, earthen compartments in which solid wastes are dumped, compacted, and covered over daily with layers of earth.

CENTRIFUGAL COLLECTOR - Any of several mechanical systems using centrifugal force to remove aerosols from a gas stream. CFS - Cubic feet per second, a measure of the amount of water passing a given point.

CHANNELIZATION - The straightening and deepening of streams to permit water to move faster, to reduce flooding, or to drain marshy acreage for farming. However, channelization reduces the organic waste assimilation capacity of the stream and may disturb fish breeding and destroy the stream's natural beauty.

CHEMICAL OXYGEN DEMAND (COD) - A measure of the amount of oxygen required to oxidize organic and oxidizable inorganic compounds in water. The COD test, like the BOD test, is used to determine the degree of pollution in an effluent.

CHEMOSTERILANT - A pesticide chemical that controls pests by destroying their ability to reproduce.

CHILLING EFFECT - The lowering of the earth's temperature due to the increase of atmospheric particulates that inhibit penetration of the sun's energy.

CHLORINATED HYDROCARBONS - A class of generally long-lasting, broad-spectrum insecticides of which the best known is DDT, first used for insect control during World War II. Other similar compounds include aldrin, dieldrin, heptachlor, chlordane, lindane, endrin, mirex, benzene hexachloride (BHC), and toxaphene. The qualities of persistence and effectivenss against a wide variety of insect pests were long regarded as highly desirable in agriculture, public health and home uses. But later research has revealed that these same qualities may represent a potential hazard through accumulation in the food chain and persistence in the environment.

CHLORINATION - The application of chlorine to drinking water, sewage or industrial waste for disinfection or oxidation of undesirable compounds.

CHLORINATOR - A device for adding a chlorine-containing gas or liquid to drinking or waste water.

CHLORINE-CONTACT CHAMBER - In a waste treatment plant, a chamber in which effluent is disinfected by chlorine before it is discharged to the receiving waters.

CHLOROSIS - Yellowing or whitening of normally green plant parts. It can be caused by disease organisms, lack of oxygen or nutrients in the soil or by various air pollutants.

CHROMIUM - (See HEAVY METALS.)

CHRONIC - Marked by long duration or frequent recurrence, as a disease.

CLARIFICATION - In waste water treatment, the removal of turbidity and suspended solids by settling, often aided by centrifugal action and chemically induced coagulation.

CLARIFIER - In waste water treatment, a settling tank which mechanically removes settleable solids from wastes.

COAGULATION - The clumping of particles in order to settle out impurities; often induced by chemicals such as lime or alum.

COASTAL ZONE - Coastal waters and adjacent lands that exert a measurable influence on the uses of the sea and its ecology.

COD - (See CHEMICAL OXYGEN DEMAND)

COEFFICIENT OF HAZE (COH) - A measurement of visibility interference in the atmosphere.

COFFIN - A thick-walled container (usually lead) used for transporting radioactive materials.

COH - (See COEFFICIENT OF HAZE)

COLIFORM INDEX - An index of the purity of water based on a count of its coliform bacteria.

COLIFORM ORGANISM - Any of a number of organisms common to the intestinal tract of man and animals whose presence in waste water is an indicator of pollution and of potentially dangerous bacterial contamination.

COMBINED SEWERS - A sewerage system that carries both sanitary sewage and storm water runoff. During dry weather, combined sewers carry all waste water to the treatment plant. During a storm, only part of the flow is intercepted because of plant overloading; the remainder goes untreated to the receiving stream.

COMBUSTION - Burning. Technically, a rapid oxidation accompanied by the release of energy in the form of heat and light. It is one of the three basic contributing factors causing air pollution; the others are attrition and vaporization.

COMMINUTION - Mechanical shredding or pulverizing of waste, a process that converts it into a homogeneous and more manageable material. Used in solid waste management and in the primary stage of waste water treatment.

COMMINUTOR - A device that grinds solids to make them easier to treat.

COMPACTION - Reducing the bulk of solid waste by rolling and tamping.

COMPOST - Relatively stable decomposed organic material.

COMPOSTING - A controlled process of degrading organic matter by microorganisms. (1) mechanical - a method in which the compost is continuously and mechanically mixed and aerated. (a) ventilated cell - compost is mixed and aerated by being dropped through a vertical series of ventilated cells. (3) windrow - an open-air method in which compostable material is placed in windrows, piles, or ventilated bins or pits and occasionally turned or mixed. The process may be anaerobic or aerobic.

CONTACT PESTICIDE - A chemical that kills pests on contact with the body, rather than by ingestion (stomach poison).

CONTRAILS - Long, narrow clouds caused by the disturbance of the atmosphere during passage of high-flying jets. Proliferation of contrails may cause changes in the weather.

COOLANT - A substance, usually liquid or gas, used for cooling any part of a reactor in which heat is generated, including the core, the reflector, shield, and other elements that may be heated by absorption of radiation.

COOLING TOWER - A device to remove excess heat from water used in industrial operations, notably in electric power generation.

CORE - The heart of a nuclear reactor where energy is released.

COVER MATERIAL - Soil that is used to cover compacted solid waste in a sanitary landfill.

CULTURAL EUTROPHICATION - Acceleration by man of the natural aging process of bodies of water.

CURIE - A measure of radiation.

CUTIE-PIE - A portable instrument equipped with a direct reading meter used to determine the level of radiation in an area.

CYCLONE COLLECTOR - A device used to collect large-size particulates from polluted air by centrifugal force.

D

DDT - The first of the modern chlorinated hydrocarbon insecticides whose chemical name is 1,1,1-tricholoro-2,2-bis (p-chloriphenyl)- ethane. It has a half-life of 15 years, and its residues can become concentrated in the fatty tissues of certain organisms, especially fish. Because of its persistence in the environment and its ability to accumulate and magnify in the food chain, EPA has banned the registration and interstate sale of DDT for nearly all uses in the United States effective December 31, 1972.

DECIBEL (dB) - A unit of sound measurement.

DECOMPOSITION - Reduction of the net energy level and change in chemical composition of organic matter because of the actions of aerobic or anaerobic microorganisms.

DERMAL TOXICITY - The ability of a pesticide chemical to poison an animal or human by skin absorption.

DESALINIZATION - Salt removal from sea or brackish water.

DESICCANT - A chemical that may be used to remove moisture from plants or insects causing them to wither and die.

DETERGENT - Synthetic washing agent that, like soap, lowers the surface tension of water, emulsifies oils and holds dirt in suspension. Environmentalists have criticized detergents because most contain large amounts of phosphorus-containing compounds that contribute to the eutrophication of waterways.

DIATOMACEOUS EARTH (DIATOMITE) - A fine siliceous material resembling chalk used in waste water treatment plants to filter sewage effluent to remove solids. May also be used as inactive ingredients in pesticide formulations applied as dust or powder.

DIFFUSED AIR - A type of sewage aeration. Air is pumped into the sewage through a perforated pipe.

DIGESTER - In a waste water treatment plant, a closed tank that decreases the volume of solids and stabilizes raw sludge by bacterial action.

DIGESTION - The biochemical decomposition of organic matter. Digestion of sewage sludge takes place in tanks where the sludge decomposes, resulting in partial gasification, liquefaction, and mineralization of pollutants.

DILUTION RATIO - The ratio of the volume of water of a stream to the volume of incoming waste. The capacity of a stream to assimilate waste is partially dependent upon the dilution ratio.

DISINFECTION - Effective killing by chemical or physical processes of all organisms capable of causing infectious diseases. Chlorination is the disinfection method commonly employed in sewage treatment processes.

DISPERSANT - A chemical agent used to break up concentrations of organic material. In cleaning oil spills, dispersants are used to disperse oil from the water surface.

DISSOLVED OXYGEN (DO) - The oxygen dissolved in water or sewage. Adequately dissolved oxygen is necessary for the life of fish and other aquatic organisms and for the prevention of offensive odors. Low dissolved oxygen concentrations generally are due to discharge of excessive organic solids having high BOD, the result of inadequate waste treatment.

DISSOLVED SOLIDS - The total amount of dissolved material, organic and inorganic, contained in water or wastes. Excessive dissolved solids make water unpalatable for drinking and unsuitable for industrial uses.

DISTILLATION - The removal of impurities from liquids by boiling. The steam, condensed back into liquid, is almost pure water; the pollutants remain in the concentrated residue.

DOSE - In radiology, the quantity of energy or radiation absorbed.

DOSIMETER (DOSEMETER) - An instrument used to measure the amount of radiation a person has received.

DREDGING - A method for deepening streams, swamps, or coastal waters by scraping and removing solids from the bottom. The resulting mud is usually deposited in marshes in a process called filling. Dredging and filling can disturb natural ecological cycles. For example, dredging can destroy oyster beds and other aquatic life; filling can destroy the feeding and breeding grounds for many fish species.

DRY LIMESTONE PROCESS - A method of controlling air pollution caused by sulfur oxides. The polluted gases are exposed to limestone which combines with oxides of sulfur to form manageable residues.

DUMP - A land site where solid waste is disposed of in a manner that does not protect the environment.

DUST - Fine-grain particulate matter that is capable of being suspended in air.

DUSTFALL JAR - An open-mouthed container used to collect large particles that fall out of the air. The particles are measured and analyzed.

DYSTROPHIC LAKES - Lakes between eutrophic and swamp stages of aging. Such lakes are shallow and have high humus content, high organic matter content, low nutrient availability, and high BOD.

E

ECOLOGICAL IMPACT - The total effect of an environmental change, either natural or man-made, on the ecology of the area.

ECOLOGY - The interrelationships of living things to one another and to their environment or the study of such interrelationships. ECONOMIC POISONS - Those chemicals used to control insects, rodents, plant diseases, weeds, and other pests, and also to defoliate economic crops such as cotton. ECOSPHERE - (See BIOSPHERE)

ECOSYSTEM - The interacting system of a biological community and its non-living environment.

EFFLUENT - A discharge of pollutants into the environment, partially or completely treated or in its natural state. Generally used in regard to discharges into waters.

ELECTRODIALYSIS - A process that uses electrical current and an arrangement of permeable membranes to separate soluble minerals from water. Often used to desalinize salt or brackish water.

ELECTROSTATIC PRECIPITATOR - An air pollution control device that removes particulate matter by imparting an electrical charge to particles in a gas stream for mechanical collection on an electrode.

EMERGENCY EPISODE - (See AIR POLLUTION EPISODE)

EMISSION - (See EFFLUENT) (Generally used in regard to discharges into air.)

EMISSION FACTOR - The average amount of a pollutant emitted from each type of polluting source in relation to a specific amount of material processed. For example, an emission factor for a blast furnace (used to make iron) would be a number of pounds of particulates per ton of raw materials.

EMISSION INVENTORY - A list of air pollutants emitted into a community's atmosphere, in amounts (usually tons) per day, by type of source. The emission inventory is basic to the establishment of emission standards.

EMISSION STANDARD - The maximum amount of a pollutant legally permitted to be discharged from a single source, either mobile or stationary.

ENRICHMENT - The addition of nitrogen, phosphorus, and carbon compounds or other nutrients into a lake or other waterway that greatly increases the growth potential for algae and other aquatic plants. Most frequently, enrichment results from the inflow of sewage effluent or from agricultural runoff.

ENVIRONMENT - The sum of all external conditions and influences affecting the life, development, and, ultimately, the survival of an organism.

ENVIRONMENTAL IMPACT STATEMENT - A document prepared by a Federal agency on the environmental impact of its proposals for legislation and other major actions significantly affecting the quality of the human environment. Environmental impact statements are used as tools for decision making and are required by the National Environmental Policy Act.

EPIDEMIOLOGY - The study of diseases as they affect populations.

EROSION - The wearing away of the land surface by wind or water. Erosion occurs naturally from weather or runoff but is often intensified by man's land-clearing practices.

ESTUARIES - Areas where the fresh water meets salt water. For example, bays, mouths of rivers, salt marshes, and lagoons. Estuaries are delicate ecosystems; they serve as nurseries, spawning and feeding grounds for a large group of marine life and provide shelter and food for birds and wildlife.

EUTROPHICATION - The normally slow aging process by which a lake evolves into a bog or marsh and ultimately assumes a completely terrestrial state and disappears. During eutrophication, the lake becomes so rich in nutritive compounds, especially nitrogen and phosphorus, that algae and other microscopic plant life becomes superabundant, thereby *choking* the lake and causing it eventually to dry up. Eutrophication may be accelerated by many human activities.

EUTROPHIC LAKES - Shallow lakes, weed-choked at the edges and very rich in nutrients. The water is characterized by large amounts of algae, low water transparency, low dissolved oxygen and high BOD.

EVAPORATION PONDS - Shallow, artificial ponds where sewage sludge is pumped, permitted to dry and either removed or buried by more sludge.

F

FABRIC FILTERS - A device for removing dust and particulate matter from industrial emissions much like a home vacuum cleaner bag. The most common use of fabric filters is the baghouse.

FECAL COLIFORM BACTERIA - A group of organisms common to the intestinal tracts of man and of animals. The presence of fecal coliform bacteria in water is an indicator of pollution and of potentially dangerous bacterial contamination.

FEEDLOT - A relatively small, confined land area for raising cattle. Although an economical method of fattening beef, feedlots concentrate a large amount of animal wastes in a small area. This excrement cannot be handled by the soil as it could be if the cattle were scattered on open range. In addition, runoff from feedlots contributes excessive quantities of nitrogen, phosphorus, and potassium to nearby waterways, thus contributing to eutrophication.

FEN - A low-lying land area partly covered by water.

FILLING - The process of depositing dirt and mud in marshy areas to create more land for real estate development. Filling can disturb natural ecological cycles. (See DREDGING)

FILM BADGE - A piece of masked photographic film worn like a badge by nuclear workers to monitor an exposure to radiation. Nuclear radiation darkens the film.

FILTRATION - In waste water treatment, the mechanical process that removes particulate matter by separating water from solid material usually by passing it through sand.

FLOC - A clump of solids formed in sewage by biological or chemical action.

FLOCCULATION - In waste water treatment, the process of separating suspended solids by chemical creation of clumps or floes.

FLOWMETER - In waste water treatment, a meter that indicates the rate at which waste water flows through the plant.

FLUE GAS - A mixture of gases resulting from combustion and emerging from a chimney. Flue gas includes nitrogen oxides, carbon oxides, water vapor, and often sulfur oxides or particulates.

FLUORIDES - Gaseous, solid or dissolved compounds containing fluorine, emitted into the air or water from a number of industrial processes. Fluorides in the air are a cause of vegetation damage and, indirectly, of livestock damage.

FLUME - A channel, either natural or manmade, which carries water.

FLY ASH - All solids, including ash, charred paper, cinders, dust, soot or other partially incinerated matter, that are carried in a gas stream.

FOG - Liquid particles formed by condensation of vaporized liquids.

FOGGING - The application of a pesticide by rapidly heating the liquid chemical, thus forming very fine droplets with the appearance of smoke. Fogging is often used to destroy mosquitoes and blackflies.

FOOD WASTE - Animal and vegetable waste resulting from the handling, storage, sale, preparation, cooking and serving of foods; commonly called garbage.

FOSSIL FUELS - Coal, oil, and natural gas; so-called because they are derived from the remains of ancient plant and animal life.

FUME - Tiny solid particles commonly formed by the condensation of vapors of solid matter.

FUMIGANT - A pesticide that is burned or evaporated to form a gas or vapor that destroys pests. Fumigants are often used in buildings or greenhouses.

FUNGI - Small, often microscopic plants without chlorophyll. Some fungi infect and cause disease in plants or animals; other fungi are useful in stabilizing sewage or in breaking down wastes for compost.

FUNGICIDE - A pesticide chemical that kills fungi or prevents them from causing diseases, usually on plants of economic importance. (See PESTICIDE)

G

GAME FISH - Those species of fish sought by sports fishermen; for example, salmon, trout, black bass, striped bass, etc. Game fish are usually more sensitive to environmental changes and water quality degradation than *rough* fish.

GAMMA RAY - Waves of radiant nuclear energy. Gamma rays are the most penetrating of the three types of radiation and are best stopped by dense materials such as lead.

GARBAGE - (See FOOD WASTE)

GARBAGE GRINDING - A method of grinding food waste by a household disposal, for example, and washing it into the sewer system. Ground garbage then must be disposed of as sewage sludge.

GEIGER COUNTER - An electrical device that detects the presence of radioactivity.

GENERATOR - A device that converts mechanical energy into electrical energy.

GERMICIDE - A chemical or agent that kills microorganisms such as bacteria and prevents them from causing disease. Such compounds must be registered as pesticides with EPA.

GRAIN - A unit of weight equivalent to 65 milligrams or 2/1,000 of an ounce.

GRAIN LOADING - The rate of emission of particulate matter from a polluting source. Measurement is made in grains of particulate matter per cubic foot of gas emitted.

GREEN BELTS - Certain areas restricted from being used for buildings and houses; they often serve as separating buffers between pollution sources and concentrations of population.

GREENHOUSE EFFECT - The heating effect of the atmosphere upon the earth. Light waves from the sun pass through the air and are absorbed by the earth. The earth then reradiates this energy as heat waves that are absorbed by the air, specifically by carbon dioxide. The air thus behaves like glass in a greenhouse, allowing the passage of light but not of heat. Thus, many scientists theorize that an increase in the atmospheric concentration of CO_2 can eventually cause an increase in the earth's surface temperature.

GROUND COVER - Grasses or other plants grown to keep soil from being blown or washed away.

GROUNDWATER - The supply of freshwater under the earth's surface in an aquifer or soil that forms the natural reservoir for man's use.

GROUNDWATER RUNOFF - Groundwater that is discharged into a stream channel as spring or seepage water.

H

HABITAT - The sum total of environmental conditions of a specific place that is occupied by an organism, a population or a community.

HALF-LIFE - The time it takes certain materials, such as persistent pesticides or radioactive isotopes, to lose half their strength. For example, the half-life of DDT is 15 years; the half-life of radium is 1,580 years.

HAMMERMILL - A broad category of high speed equipment that uses pivoted or fixed hammers or cutters to crush, grind, chip, or shred solid wastes.

HARD WATER - Water containing dissolved minerals such as calcium, iron, and magnesium. The most notable characteristic of hard water is its inability to lather soap. Some pesticide chemicals will curdle or settle out when added to hard water.

HAZARDOUS AIR POLLUTANT - According to law, a pollutant to which no ambient air quality standard is applicable and that may cause or contribute to an increase in mortality or in serious illness. For example, asbestos, beryllium, and mercury have been declared hazardous air pollutants.

HEAT ISLAND EFFECT - An air circulation problem peculiar to cities. Tall buildings, heat from pavements, and concentrations of pollutants create a haze dome that prevents rising hot air from being cooled at its normal rate. A self-contained circulation system is put in motion that can be broken by relatively strong winds. If such winds are absent, the heat island can trap high concentrations of pollutants and present a serious health problem.

HEATING SYSTEM - The coldest months of the year when pollution emissions are higher in some areas because of increased fossil-fuel consumption.

HEAVY METALS - Metallic elements with high molecular weights, generally toxic in low concentrations to plant and animal life. Such metals are often residual in the environment and exhibit biological accumulation. Examples include mercury, chromium, calcium, arsenic, and lead.

HERBICIDE - A pesticide chemical used to destroy or control the growth of weeds, bush, and other undesirable plants. (See PESTICIDE)

HERBIVORE - An organism that feeds on vegetation.

HETEROTROPHIC ORGANISM - Organisms dependent on organic matter for food.

HIGH DENSITY POLYETHYLENE - A material often used in the manufacture of plastic bottles that produces toxic fumes if incinerated.

HI-VOLUME SAMPLER - A device used in the measurement and analysis of suspended particulate pollution. Also called a Hi-Vol.

HOT - A colloquial term meaning highly radioactive.

HUMUS - Decomposed organic material.

HYDROCARBONS - A vast family of compounds containing carbon and hydrogen in various combinations, found especially in fossil fuels. Some hydrocarbons are major air pollutants, some may be carcinogenic and others contribute to photochemical smog.

HYDROGEN SULFIDE (H_2S) - A malodorous gas made up of hydrogen and sulfur with the characteristic odor of rotten eggs. It is emitted in the natural decomposition of organic matter and is also the natural accompaniment of advanced stages of eutrophication. H_2S is also a byproduct of refinery activity and the combusion of oil during power plant operations. In heavy concentrations, it can cause illness.

HYDROLOGY - The science dealing with the properties, distribution, and circulation of water and snow.

I

IMPEDANCE - The rate at which a substance can absorb and transmit sound.

IMPLEMENTATION PLAN - A document of the steps to be taken to ensure attainment of environmental quality standards within a specified time period. Implementation plans are required by various laws.

IMPOUNDMENT - A body of water, such as a pond, confined by a dam, dike, floodgate, or other barrier.

INCINERATION - The controlled process by which solid, liquid, or gaseous combustible wastes are burned and changed into gases; the residue produced contains little or no combustible material.

INCINERATOR - An engineered apparatus used to burn waste substances and in which all the combustion factors - temperature, retention time, turbulence, and combusion air - can be controlled.

INERT GAS - A gas that does not react with other substances under ordinary conditions.

INERTIAL SEPARATOR - An air pollution control device that uses the principle of inertia to remove particulate matter from a stream of air or gas.

INFILTRATION - The flow of a fluid into a substance through pores or small openings. Commonly used in hydrology to denote the flow of water into soil material.

INOCULUM - Material such as bacteria placed in compost or other medium to initiate biological action.

INTEGRATED PEST CONTROL - A system of managing pests by using biological, cultural, and chemical means.

INTERCEPTOR SEWERS - Sewers used to collect the flows from main and trunk sewers and carry them to a central point for treatment and discharge. In a combined sewer system, where street runoff from rains is allowed to enter the system along with sewage, interceptor sewers allow some of the sewage to flow untreated directly into the receiving stream, to prevent the plant from being overloaded.

INTERSTATE CARRIER WATER SUPPLY - A water supply whose water may be used for drinking or cooking purposes aboard common carriers (planes, trains, buses, and ships) operating interstate. Interstate carrier water supplies are regulated by the Federal government.

INTERSTATE WATERS - According to law, waters defined as (1) rivers, lakes and other waters that flow across or form a part of state or international boundaries; (2) waters of the Great Lakes; (3) coastal waters - whose scope has been defined to include ocean waters seaward to the territorial limits and waters along the coastline (including inland streams) influenced by the tide.

INVERSION - An atmospheric condition where a layer of cool air is trapped by a layer of warm air so that it cannot rise. Inversions spread polluted air horizontally rather than vertically so that contaminating substances cannot be widely dispersed. An inversion of several days can cause an air pollution episode.

IONIZATION CHAMBER - A device roughly similar to a geiger counter that reveals the presence of ionizing radiation.

ISOTOPE - A variation of an element having the same atomic number as the element itself, but having a different atomic weight because of a different number of neutrons. Different isotopes of the same element have different radioactive behavior.

L

LAGOON - In waste water treatment, a shallow pond usually man-made where sunlight, bacterial action, and oxygen interact to restore waste water to a reasonable state of purity.

LATERAL SEWERS - Pipes running underneath city streets that collect sewage from homes or businesses.

LC_{50} - Median lethal concentration, a standard measure of toxicity.

LC_{50} indicates the concentration of a substance that will kill 50 percent of a group of experimental insects or animals.

LEACHATE - Liquid that has percolated through solid waste or other mediums and has extracted dissolved or suspended materials from it.

LEACHING - The process by which soluble materials in the soil, such as nutrients, pesticide chemicals or contaminants, are washed into a lower layer of soil or are dissolved and carried away by water.

LEAD - A heavy metal that may be hazardous to human health if breathed or ingested.

LIFE CYCLE - The phases, changes or stages an organism passes through during its lifetime.

LIFT - In a sanitary landfill, a compacted layer of solid waste and the top layer of cover material.

LIMNOLOGY - The study of the physical, chemical, meteorological, and biological aspects of fresh waters.

M

MARSH - A low-lying tract of soft, wet land that provides an important ecosystem for a variety of plant and animal life but often is destroyed by dredging and filling.

MASKING - Covering over of one sound or element by another. Quantitatively, masking is the amount of audibility threshold of one sound is raised by the presence of a second masking sound. Also used in regard to odors.

MECHANICAL TURBULENCE - The erratic movement of air caused by local obstructions, such as buildings.

MERCURY - A heavy metal, highly toxic if breathed or ingested. Mercury is residual in the environment, showing biological accumulation in all aquatic organisms, especially fish and shellfish. Chronic exposure to airborne mercury can have serious effect on the central nervous system.

METHANE - Colorless, nonpoisonous, and flammable gaseous hydrocarbon. Methane (CA) is emitted by marshes and by dumps undergoing anaerobic decomposition.

MOD - Millions of gallons per day. Mgd is commonly used to express rate of flow.

MICROBES - Minute plant or animal life. Some disease-causing microbes exist in sewage.

MIST - Liquid particles in air formed by condensation of vaporized liquids. Mist particles vary from 500 to 40 microns in size. By comparison, fog particles are smaller than 40 microns in size. MIXED LIQUOR - A mixture of activated sludge and water containing organic matter undergoing activated sludge treatment in the aeration tank.

MOBILE SOURCE - A moving source of air pollution such as an automobile.

MONITORING - Periodic or continuous determination of the amount of pollutants or radioactive contamination present in the environment.

MUCK SOILS - Soils made from decaying plant materials.

MULCH - A layer of wood chips, dry leaves, straw, hay, plastic strips or other material placed on the soil around plants to retain moisture, to prevent weeds from growing, and to enrich soil.

N

NATURAL GAS - A fuel gas occurring naturally in certain geologic formation. Natural gas is usually a combustible mixture of methane and hydrocarbons.

NATURAL SELECTION - The natural process by which the organisms best adapted to their environment survive and those less well adapted are eliminated.

NECROSIS - Death of plant cells resulting in a discolored, sunken area or death of the entire plant.

NITRIC OXIDE (NO) - A gas formed in great part from atmospheric nitrogen and oxygen when combustion takes place under high temperature and high pressure, as in internal combustion engines. NO is not itself a pollutant; however, in the ambient air, it converts to nitrogen dioxide, a major contributor to photochemical smog.

NITROGEN DIOXIDE (NO_2) - A compound produced by the oxidation of nitric oxide in the atmosphere; a major contributor to photochemical smog.

NITROGENOUS WASTES - Wastes of animal or plant origin that contain a significant concentration of nitrogen.

NO - A notation meaning oxides of nitrogen. (See NITRIC OXIDE)

NOISE - Any undesired audible signal. Thus, in acoustics, noise is any undesired sound.

NTA - Nitrilotriacetic acid, a compound once used to replace phosphates in detergents.

NUCLEAR POWER PLANT - Any device, machine, or assembly that converts nuclear energy into some form of useful power, such as mechanical or electrical power. In a nuclear electric power plant, heat produced by a reactor is generally used to make steam to drive a turbine that in turn drives an electric generator.

NUTRIENTS - Elements or compounds essential as raw materials for organism growth and development; for example, carbon, oxygen, nitrogen, and phosphorus.

<u>O</u>

OIL SPILL - The accidental discharge of oil into oceans, bays or inland waterways. Methods of oil spill control include chemical dispersion, combustion, mechanical containment, and absorption.

OLIGOTROPHIC LAKES - Deep lakes that have a low supply of nutrients and thus contain little organic matter. Such lakes are characterized by high water transparency and high dissolved oxygen. OPACITY - Degree of obscuration of light. For example, a window has zero opacity; a wall is 100 percent opaque. The Ringelmann system of evaluating smoke density is based on opacity. OPEN BURNING - Uncontrolled burning of wastes in an open dump.

OPEN DUMP - (See DUMP)

ORGANIC - Referring to or derived from living organisms. In chemistry, any compound containing carbon.

ORGANISM - Any living human, plant or animal.

ORGANOPHOSPHATES - A group of pesticide chemicals containing phosphorus, such as malathion and parathion, intended to control insects. These compounds are short-lived and, therefore, do not normally contaminate the environment. However, some organophosphates, such as parathion, are extremely toxic when initially applied and exposure to them can interfere with the normal processes of the nervous system, causing convulsions and eventually death. Malathion, on the other hand, is low in toxicity and relatively safe for humans and animals. It is a common ingredient in household insecticide products.

OUTFALL - The mouth of a sewer, drain or conduit where an effluent is discharged into the receiving waters.

OVERFIRE AIR - Air forced into the top of an incinerator to fan the flame.

OXIDANT - Any oxygen containing substance that reacts chemically in the air to produce new substances. Oxidants are the primary contributors to photochemical smog.

OXIDATION - A chemical reaction in which oxygen unites or combines with other elements. Organic matter is oxidized by the action of aerobic bacteria; thus, oxidation is used in waste water treatment to break down organic wastes.

OXIDATION POND - A man-made lake or pond in which organic wastes are reduced by bacterial action. Often oxygen is bubbled through the pond to speed the process.

OZONE (O_2) - A pungent, colorless, toxic gas. Ozone is one component of photochemical smog and is considered a major air pollutant.

<u>P</u>

PACKAGE PLANT - A prefabricated or prebuilt waste water treatment plant.

PACKED TOWER - An air pollution control device in which polluted air is forced upward through a tower packed with crushed rock or wood chips while the liquid is sprayed downward on the packing material. The pollutants in the air stream either dissolve or chemically react with the liquid.

PAN - Peroxyacetyl nitrate, a pollutant created by the action of sunlight on hydrocarbons and nitrogen oxides in the air. PANS are an integral part of photochemical smog.

PARTICULATES - Finely divided solid or liquid particles in the air or in air emission. Particulates include dust, smoke, fumes, mist, spray, and fog.

PARTICULATE LOADING - The introduction of particulates into the ambient air.

PATHOGENIC - Causing or capable of causing disease.

PCBs - Polychlorinated biphenyls, a group of organic compounds used in the manufacture of plastics. In the environment, PCBs exhibit many of the same characteristics as DDT and may, therefore, be confused with that pesticide. PCBs are highly toxic to aquatic life; they persist in the environment for long periods of time, and they are biologically accumulative.

PEAT - Partially decomposed organic material.

PERCOLATION - Downward flow or infiltration of water through the pores or spaces of a rock or soil.

PERSISTENT PESTICIDES - Pesticides that will be present in the environment for longer than one growing season or one year after application.

PESTICIDE - An agent used to control pests. This includes insecticides for use against harmful insects, herbicides for weed control, fungicides for control of plant diseases, rodenticides for killing rats, mice, etc., and germicides used in disinfectant products, algaecides, slimicides, etc. Some pesticides can contaminate water, air or soil and accumulate in man, animals, and the environment, particularly if they are misused. Certain of these chemicals have been shown to interfere with the reproductive processes of predatory birds and possibly other animals.

PESTICIDE TOLERANCE - A scientifically and legally established limit for the amount of chemical residue that can be permitted to remain in or on a harvested food or feed crop as a result of the application of a chemical for pest-control purposes. Such tolerances or safety levels, established federally by EPA, are set well below the point at which residues might be harmful to consumers.

pH - A measure of the acidity or alkalinity of a material, liquid, or solid. pH is represented on a scale of 0 to 14, with 7 representing a neutral state, 0 representing the most acid and 14, the most alkaline.

PHENOLS - A group of organic compounds that in very low concentrations produce a taste and odor problem in water. In higher concentrations, they are toxic to aquatic life. Phenols are byproducts of petroleum refining, tanning and textile, dye and resin manufacture.

PHOSPHORUS - An element that, while essential to life, contributes to the eutrophication of lakes and other bodies of water.

PHOTOCHEMICAL OXIDANTS - Secondary pollutants formed by the action of nitrogen and hydrocarbons in the air; they are the primary contributors to photochemical smog.

PHOTOCHEMICAL SMOG - Air pollution associated with oxidants rather than with sulfur oxides, particulates, etc. Produces necrosis, chlorosis, and growth alterations in plants and is an eye and respiratory irritant in humans.

PHYTOPLANKTON - The plant portion of plankton.

PHYTOTOXIC - Injurious to plants.

PIG - A container usually made of lead used to ship or store radioactive materials.

PILE - A nuclear reactor.

PLANKTON - The floating or weakly swimming plant and animal life in a body of water, often microscopic in size.

PLUME - The visible emission from a flue or chimney.

POINT SOURCE - In air pollution, a stationary source of a large individual emission, generally of an industrial nature. This is a general definition; point source is legally and precisely defined in Federal regulations. (See AREA SOURCE)

POLLEN - A fine dust produced by plants; a natural or background air pollutant.

POLLUTANT - Any introduced gas, liquid or solid that makes a resource unfit for a specific purpose.

POLLUTION - The presence of matter or energy whose nature, location, or quantity produces undesired environmental effects.

POLYELECTROLYTES - Synthetic chemicals used to speed flocculation of solids in sewage.

POTABLE WATER - Water suitable for drinking or cooking purposes from both health and aesthetic considerations.

PPM - Parts per million. The unit commonly used to represent the degree of pollutant concentration where the concentrations are small. Larger concentrations are given in percentages. Thus, BOD is represented in ppm, while suspended solids in water are expressed in percentages. In air, ppm is usually a volume/volume ratio; in water, a weight/volume ratio.

PRECIPITATE - A solid that separates from a solution because of some chemical or physical change or the formation of such a solid.

PRECIPITATORS - In pollution control work, any of a number of air pollution control devices usually using mechanical/electrical means to collect particulates from an emission.

PRETREATMENT - In waste water treatment, any process used to reduce pollution load before the waste water is introduced into a main sewer system or delivered to a treatment plant for substantial reduction of the pollution load.

PRIMARY TREATMENT - The first stage in waste water treatment in which substantially all floating or settleable solids are mechanically removed by screening and sedimentation.

PROCESS WEIGHT - The total weight of all materials, including fuels, introduced into a manufacturing process. The process weight is used to calculate the allowable rate of emission of pollutant matter from the process.

PULVERIZATION - The crushing or grinding of material into small pieces.

PUMPING STATION - A station at which sewage is pumped to a higher level. In most sewer systems, pumping is unnecessary; waste water flows by gravity to the treatment plant.

PUTRESCIBLE - Capable of being decomposed by microorganisms with sufficient rapidity to cause nuisances from odors, gases, etc. For example, kitchen wastes or dead animals.

Q

QUENCH TANK - A water-filled tank used to cool incinerator residues.

R

RAD - A unit of measurement of any kind of radiation absorbed by man.

RADIATION - The emission of fast atomic particles or rays by the nucleus of an atom. Some elements are naturally radioactive while others become radioactive after bombardment with neutrons or other particles. The three major forms of radiation are alpha, beta, and gamma.

RADIATION STANDARDS - Regulations that include exposure standards, permissible concentrations and regulations for transportation.

RADIOBIOLOGY - The study of the principles, mechanisms, and effects of radiation on living matter.

RADIOECOLOGY - The study of the effects of radiation on species of plants and animals in natural communities.

RADIOISOTOPES - Radioactive isotopes. Radioisotopes, such as cobalt-60, are used in the treatment of disease.

RASP - A device used to grate solid waste into a more manageable material, ridding it of much of its odor.

RAW SEWAGE - Untreated domestic or commercial waste water.

RECEIVING WATERS - Rivers, lakes, oceans, or other bodies that receive treated or untreated waste waters.

RECYCLING - The process by which waste materials are transformed into new products in such a manner that the original products may lose their identity.

RED TIDE - A proliferation or bloom of a certain type of plankton with red-to-orange coloration, that often causes massive fish kills. Though they are a natural phenomenon, blooms are believed to be stimulated by phosphorus and other nutrients discharged into waterways by man.

REFUSE - (See SOLID WASTE)

REFUSE RECLAMATION - The process of converting solid waste to saleable products. For example, the composting of organic solid waste yields a saleable soil conditioner.

REM - A measurement of radiation dose to the internal tissues of man.

REP - A unit of measurement of any kind of radiation absorbed by man.

RESERVOIR - A pond, lake, tank, or basin, natural or man-made, used for the storage, regulation, and control of water.

RESOURCE RECOVERY - The process of obtaining materials or energy, particularly from solid waste.

REVERBERATION - The persistence of sound in an enclosed space after the sound source has stopped.

RINGELMANN CHART - A series of illustrations ranging from light grey to black used to measure the opacity of smoke emitted from stacks and other sources. The shades of grey simulate various moke densities and are assigned numbers ranging from one to five. Ringelmann No. 1 is equivalent to 20 percent dense; No. 5 is 100 percent dense. Ringelmann charts are used in the setting and enforcement of emission standards.

RIPARIAN RIGHTS - Rights of a land owner to the water on or bordering his property, including the right to prevent diversion or misuse of upstream water.

RIVER BASIN - The total area drained by a river and its tributaries.

RODENTICIDE - A chemical or agent used to destroy or prevent damage by rats or other rodent pests. (See PESTICIDE)

ROUGH FISH - Those fish species considered to be of poor fighting quality when taken on tackle or of poor eating quality; for example, gar, suckers, etc. Most rough fish are more tolerant of widely changing environmental conditions than are game fish.

RUBBISH - A general term for solid waste, excluding food waste and ashes, taken from residences, commercial establishments, and institutions.

RUNOFF - The portion of rainfall, melted snow, or irrigation water that flows across ground surface and eventually is returned to streams. Runoff can pick up pollutants from the air or the land and carry them to the receiving waters.

S

SALINITY - The degree of salt in water.

SALT WATER INTRUSION - The invasion of salt water into a body of fresh water, occurring in either surface or groundwater bodies. When this invasion is caused by oceanic waters, it is called sea water intrusion.

SALVAGE - The utilization of waste materials.

SANITATION - The control of all the factors in man's physical environment that exercise or can exercise a deleterious effect on his physical development, health, and survival.

SANITARY LANDFILL - A site for solid waste disposal using sanitary landfilling techniques.

SANITARY LANDFILLING - An engineered method of solid waste disposal on land in a manner that protects the environment; waste is spread in thin layers, compacted to the smallest practical volume and covered with soil at the end of each working day. SANITARY SEWERS - Sewers that carry only domestic or commercial sewage. Storm water runoff is carried in a separate system. (See SEWER)

SCRAP - Discarded or rejected materials that result from manufacturing or fabricating operations and are suitable for reprocessing.

SCREENING - The removal of relatively coarse floating and suspended solids by straining through racks or screens.

SCRUBBER - An air pollution control device that uses a liquid spray to remove pollutants from a gas stream by absorption or chemical reaction. Scrubbers also reduce the temperature of the emission.

SECONDARY TREATMENT - Waste water treatment, beyond the primary stage, in which bacteria consume the organic parts of the wastes. This biochemical action is accomplished by use of trickling filters or the activated sludge process. Effective secondary treatment removes virtually all floating and settleable solids and approximately 90 percent of both BOD_3 and suspended solids. Customarily, disinfection by chlorination is the final stage of the secondary treatment process.

SEDIMENTATION - In waste water treatment, the settling out of solids by gravity.

SEDIMENTATION TANKS - In waste water treatment, tanks where the solids are allowed to settle or to float as scum. Scum is skimmed off; settled solids are pumped to incinerators, digesters, filters, or other means of disposal.

SEEPAGE - Water that flows through the soil.

SELECTIVE HERBICIDE - A pesticide intended to kill only certain types of plants, especially broad-leafed weeds, and not harm other plants such as farm crops or lawn grasses. The leading herbicide in the United States is 2,4-D. A related but stronger chemical used mostly for brush control on range, pasture, and forest lands and on utility or highway rights-of-way is 2,4,5-T. Uses of the latter chemical have been somewhat restricted because of laboratory evidence that it or a dioxin contaminant in 2,4,5-T can cause birth defects in test animals.

SENESCENCE - The process of growing old. Sometimes used to refer to lakes nearing extinction.

SEPTIC TANK - An underground tank used for the deposition of domestic wastes. Bacteria in the wastes decompose the organic matter, and the sludge settles to the bottom. The effluent flows through drains into the ground. Sludge is pumped out at regular intervals.

SETTLEABLE SOLIDS - Bits of debris and fine matter heavy enough to settle out of waste water.

SETTLING CHAMBER - In air pollution control, a low-cost device used to reduce the velocity of flue gases usually by means of baffles, promoting the settling of fly ash.

SETTLING TANK - In waste water treatment, a tank or basin in which settleable solids are removed by gravity.

SEWAGE - The total of organic waste and waste water generated by residential and commercial establishments.

SEWAGE LAGOON - (See LAGOON)

SEWER - Any pipe or conduit used to collect and carry away sewage or storm water runoff from the generating source to treatment plants or receiving streams. A sewer that conveys household and commercial sewage is called a sanitary sewer. If it transports runoff from rain or snow, it is called a storm sewer. Often storm water runoff and sewage are transported in the same system or combined sewers.

SEWERAGE - The entire system of sewage collection, treatment, and disposal. Also applies to all effluent carried by sewers, whether it is sanitary sewage, industrial wastes, or storm water runoff.

SHIELD - A wall that protects workers from harmful radiation released by radioactive materials.

SILT - Finely divided particles of soil or rock. Often carried in cloudy suspension in water and eventually deposited as sediment.

SINKING - A method of controlling oil spills that employs an agent to entrap oil droplets and sink them to the bottom of the body of water. The oil and sinking agent are eventually biologically degraded.

SKIMMING - The mechanical removal of oil or scum from the surface of water.

SLUDGE - The construction of solids removed from sewage during waste water treatment. Sludge disposal is then handled by incineration, dumping, or burial.

SMOG - Generally used as an equivalent of air pollution, particularly associated with oxidants.

SMOKE - Solid particles generated as a result of the incomplete combustion of materials containing carbon.

SO_x - A symbol meaning oxides of sulfur.

SOFT DETERGENTS - Biodegradable detergents.

SOIL CONDITIONER - A biologically stable organic material such as humus or compost that makes soil more amenable to the passage of water and to the distribution of fertilizing material, providing a better medium for necessary soil bacteria growth.

SOLID WASTE - Useless, unwanted or discarded material with insufficient liquid content to be free flowing. Also see WASTE. (1)

    (1) Agricultural - solid waste that results from the raising and slaughtering of animals, and the processing of animal products and orchard and field crops.

    (2) Commercial - waste generated by stores, offices, and other activities that do not actually turn out a product.

    (3) Industrial - waste that results from industrial processes and manufacturing.

    (4) Institutional - waste originating from educational, health care, and research facilities.

    (5) Municipal - residential and commercial solid waste generated within a community.

    (6) Pesticide - the residue from the manufacturing, handling or use of chemicals intended for killing plant and animal pests.

    (7) Residential - waste that normally originates in a residential environment. Sometimes called domestic solid waste.

SOLID WASTE DISPOSAL - The ultimate disposition of refuse that cannot be salvaged or recycled.

SOLID WASTE MANAGEMENT - The purposeful, systematic control of the generation, storage, collection, transport, separation, processing, recycling, recovery, and disposal of solid wastes.

SONIC BOOM - The tremendous booming sound produced as a vehicle, usually a supersonic jet airplane, exceeds the speed of sound, and the shock wave reaches the ground.

SOOT - Agglomerations of tar-impregnated carbon particles that form when carbonaceous material does not undergo complete combustion.

SORPTION - A term including both adsorption and absorption. Sorption is basic to many processes used to remove gaseous and particulate pollutants from an emission and to clean up oil spills.

SPOIL - Dirt or rock that has been removed from its original location, specifically materials that have been dredged from the bottom of waterways.

STABILIZATION - The process of converting active organic matter in sewage sludge or solid wastes into inert, harmless material.

STABILIZATION PONDS - (See LAGOON, OXIDATION POND)

STABLE AIR - An air mass that remains in the same position rather than moving in its normal horizontal and vertical directions. Stable air does not disperse pollutants and can lead to high build-ups of air pollution.

STACK - A smokestack; a vertical pipe or flue designed to exhaust gases and suspended particulate matter.

STACK EFFECT - The upward movement of hot gases in a stack due to the temperature difference between the gases and the atmosphere.

STAGNATION - Lack of wind in an air mass or lack of motion in water. Both cases tend to entrap and concentrate pollutants.

STATIONARY SOURCE - A pollution emitter that is fixed rather than moving as an automobile.

STORM SEWER - A conduit that collects and transports rain and snow runoff back to the ground water. In a separate sewerage system, storm sewers are entirely separate from those carrying domestic and commercial waste water.

STRATIFICATION - Separating into layers.

STRIP MINING - A process in which rock and top soil strat overlying ore or fuel deposits are scraped away by mechanical shovels. Also known as surface mining.

SULFUR DIOXIDE

(SO_2) - A heavy, pungent, colorless gas formed primarily by the combustion of fossil fuels. SO_2 damages the respiratory tract as well as vegetation and materials and is considered a major air pollutant.

SUMP - A depression or tank that serves as a drain or receptacle for liquids for salvage or disposal.

SURFACTANT - An agent used in detergents to cause lathering. Composed of several phosphate compounds, surfactants are a source of external enrichment thought to speed the eutrophication of our lakes.

SURVEILLANCE SYSTEM - A monitoring system to determine environmental quality. Surveillance systems should be established to monitor all aspects of progress toward attainment of environmental standards and to identify potential episodes of high pollutant concentrations in time to take preventive action.

SUSPENDED SOLIDS (SS) - Small particles of solid pollutants in sewage that contribute to turbidity and that resist separation by conventional means. The examination of suspended solids and the BOD test constitute the two main determinations for water quality performed at waste water treatment facilities.

SYNERGISM - The cooperative action of separate substances so that the total effect is greater than the sum of the effects of the substances acting independently.

SYSTEMIC PESTICIDE - A pesticide chemical that is carried to other parts of a plant or animal after it is injected or taken up from the soil or body surface.

T

TAILINGS - Second grade or waste material derived when raw material is screened or processed.

TERTIARY TREATMENT - Waste water treatment beyond the secondary or biological stage that includes removal of nutrients such as phosphorus and nitrogen and a high percentage of suspended solids. Tertiary treatment, also known as advanced waste treatment, produces a high quality effluent.

THERMAL POLLUTION - Degradation of water quality by the introduction of the heated effluent. Primarily a result of the discharge of cooling waters from industrial processes, particularly from electrical power generation. Even small deviations from normal water temperatures can affect aquatic life. Thermal pollution usually can be controlled by cooling towers.

THRESHOLD DOSE - The minimum dose of given substance necessary to produce a measurable physiological or psychological effect.

TOLERANCE - The relative capability of an organism to endure an unfavorable environmental factor. The amount of a chemical considered safe on any food to be eaten by man or animals. (See PESTICIDE TOLERANCE)

TOPOGRAPHY - The configuration of a surface area including its relief or relative elevations and the position of its natural and man-made features.

TOXICANT - A substance that kills or injures an organism through its chemical or physical action or by altering its environment; for example, cyanides, phenols, pesticides or heavy metals. Especially used for insect control.

TOXICITY - The quality or degree of being poisonous or harmful to plant or animal life.

TRICKLING FILTER - A device for the biological or secondary treatment of waste water consisting of a bed of rocks or stones that support bacterial growth. Sewage is trickled over the bed, enabling the bacteria to break down organic wastes.

TROPOSPHERE - The layer of the atmosphere extending seven to ten miles above the earth. Vital to life on earth, it contains clouds and moisture that reach earth as rain or snow.

TURBIDIMETER - A device used to measure the amount of suspended solids in a liquid.

TURBIDITY - A thick, hazy condition of air due to the presence of particulates or other pollutants, or the similar cloudy condition in water due to the suspension of silt or finely divided organic matter.

U

URBAN RUNOFF - Storm water from city streets and gutters that usually contains a great deal of litter and organic and bacterial wastes.

V

VAPOR - The gaseous phase of substances that normally are either liquids or solids at atmospheric temperature and pressure; for example, steam and phenolic compounds.

VAPOR PLUME - The stack effluent consisting of flue gas made visible by condensed water droplets or mist.

VAPORIZATION - The change of a substance from the liquid to the gaseous state. One of three basic contributing factors to air pollution; the others are attrition and combustion.

VARIANCE - Sanction granted by a governing body for delay or exception in the application of a given law, ordinance, or regulation.

VECTOR - Disease vector - a carrier, usually an arthropod, that is capable of transmitting a pathogen from one organism to another.

VOLATILE - Evaporating readily at a relatively low temperature.

W

WASTE - Also see SOLID WASTE.

(1) Bulky waste - items whose large size precludes or complicates their handling by normal collection, processing, or disposal methods.

(2) Construction and demolition waste - building materials and rubble resulting from construction, remodeling, repair, and demolition operations.

(3) Hazardous waste - wastes that require special handling to avoid illness or injury to persons or damage to property.

(4) Special waste - those wastes that require extraordinary management.

(5) Wood pulp waste - wood or paper fiber residue resulting from a manufacturing process.

(6) Yard waste - plant clippings, prunings, and other discarded material from yards and gardens. Also known as yard rubbish.

WASTE WATER - Water carrying wastes from homes, businesses, and industries that is a mixture of water and dissolved or suspended solids.

WATER POLLUTION - The addition of sewage, industrial wastes, or other harmful or objectionable material to water in concentrations or in sufficient quantities to result in measurable degradation of water quality.

WATER QUALITY CRITERIA - The levels of pollutants that affect the suitability of water for a given use. Generally, water use classification includes: public water supply, recreation, propagation of fish and other aquatic life, agricultural use and industrial use.

WATER QUALITY STANDARD - A plan for water quality management containing four major elements: the use (recreation, drinking water, fish and wildlife propagation, industrial, or agricultural) to be made of the water; criteria to protect those uses; implementation plans (for needed industrial-municipal waste treatment improvements); and enforcement plans, and on anti-degration statement to protect existing high quality waters.

WATERSHED - The area drained by a given stream.

WATER SUPPLY SYSTEM - The system for the collection, treatment, storage, and distribution of potable water from the sources of supply to the consumer.

WATER TABLE - The upper level of ground water.

Z

ZOOPLANKTON - Planktonic animals that supply food for fish.

CPSIA information can be obtained
at www.ICGtesting.com
Printed in the USA
BVHW011429171219
566926BV00012B/384/P